# BOLIVIA

## UNVEILED 2025

**HUDSON MYRON**

# TABLE OF CONTENTS

# WELCOME TO BOLIVIA

Imagine waking up to the crisp, cool air of the Andes, the sun gently rising over snow-capped peaks, casting a golden glow on the sprawling city of La Paz far below. You step outside, feeling the altitude tug at your breath, and for a moment, it hits you: you're standing in one of the most unique places on Earth. Welcome to Bolivia, a country that seems to defy logic and expectation at every turn, a place where time moves at its own pace and where history, culture, and nature collide in the most spectacular ways.

Your journey begins as many others have – with a sense of wonder and a heart full of questions. What lies beyond the bustling streets of La Paz? What stories do the ancient stones of Tiwanaku whisper to those who listen? And what secrets does the vast, shimmering expanse of Salar de Uyuni hold beneath its mirror-like surface?

As you explore Bolivia, you realize that this land is more than a destination – it's a living, breathing experience that challenges the traveler in ways both subtle and profound. Bolivia isn't just a place you visit, it's a place you feel, a land where every corner offers something new and unexpected. The towering Andes give way to the lush green depths of the Amazon Basin, while the vast Altiplano stretches endlessly into the horizon, dotted with llama herders and vibrant indigenous villages.

Bolivia is a land of contrasts, where high-altitude deserts meet cloud forests, and ancient traditions coexist with modern life. One day, you find yourself wandering through the colonial streets of Sucre, where whitewashed buildings and cobblestone streets tell tales of Spanish conquest and revolution. The next, you're navigating the untamed wilderness of Madidi National Park, where jaguars roam freely, and howler monkeys echo through the trees. The journey is both humbling and exhilarating, as Bolivia continually reminds you of the raw power and beauty of nature.

And then there's the people. Bolivia's heart beats strongest in the warmth of its people, who carry centuries of history in their blood. The indigenous cultures here are among the oldest in South America, and everywhere you go, you encounter vibrant traditions that have stood the test of time. Whether you're bargaining at the bustling markets of Cochabamba, joining in the colorful dances of the Oruro

Carnival, or learning the art of weaving from a Quechua artisan, you begin to see Bolivia not just as a destination, but as a story – one that has been unfolding for thousands of years.

But Bolivia is also a place of challenges. The high altitude can take your breath away – both literally and figuratively – and the roads that wind through the mountains can test even the most adventurous of travelers. Yet, it's in these moments that Bolivia reveals its true magic. For those willing to embrace the unexpected, to lose themselves in the experience, Bolivia offers a reward unlike any other.

The shimmering beauty of the Uyuni Salt Flats, the mystical waters of Lake Titicaca, the haunting ruins of Tiwanaku – these are places that stay with you long after you've left. They're more than just landmarks; they're reminders of the vastness of the world, of the incredible diversity that exists within it, and of the journeys we take not only through physical space, but through culture, history, and even within ourselves.

As you prepare for your own journey through Bolivia, this guide is here to help you navigate the wonders and mysteries of this incredible country. Inside, you'll find practical tips, hidden gems, and insider advice to make your adventure unforgettable. Whether you're trekking through the wild landscapes of the Andes, exploring ancient ruins, or immersing yourself in the vibrant rhythms of Bolivian festivals, we'll guide you through every step of the way.

Bolivia is a land that leaves its mark on all who visit. It's a place where adventure meets reflection, where the past and present blend seamlessly, and where every traveler becomes part of the story. As you set out on this adventure, prepare to be challenged, inspired, and transformed.

Welcome to Bolivia. Your journey is just beginning.

# BEST TIMES TO VISIT

When planning a journey to Bolivia, timing can make all the difference. With its diverse geography—from the towering peaks of the Andes to the lush Amazon Basin—Bolivia experiences a wide range of climates, each offering a unique experience for travelers. Whether you're chasing clear skies over the shimmering salt flats of Salar de Uyuni or hoping to explore the Amazon jungle at its most vibrant, understanding Bolivia's seasons is key to making the most of your adventure.

**Bolivia's Seasons:** Bolivia's climate is largely shaped by two distinct seasons: the dry season (May to October) and the wet season (November to April). These seasons affect not just the weather but also the accessibility and appearance of many of the country's natural wonders. Choosing the best time to visit depends on the kind of experience you're seeking, as each season offers its own advantages.

**Dry Season (May to October):** For most travelers, the dry season is considered the best time to visit Bolivia, especially if your itinerary includes iconic destinations like the Salar de Uyuni, La Paz, or Lake Titicaca. During these months, the weather is generally cooler and more stable, with clear skies and less rainfall, making it ideal for outdoor activities and exploration.

1. **Clear Skies and Stunning Views:** One of the main draws of the dry season is the consistent sunshine and blue skies, which create perfect conditions for exploring Bolivia's high-altitude landscapes. In the Altiplano (the high plateau region), you'll find cooler temperatures that make hiking and trekking more comfortable. Popular treks, such as the El Choro Trail or the ascent of Huayna Potosí, are much more enjoyable in dry conditions, with less risk of sudden rainstorms or muddy trails.

2. **Exploring the Salar de Uyuni:** The dry season is also the best time to experience the Salar de Uyuni, the world's largest salt flat. During these months, the salt flats take on their iconic white, crystalline appearance, stretching endlessly toward the horizon. It's the perfect time for photography, as the salt flats create otherworldly landscapes that seem to defy reality.

Travelers can also explore the unique salt hotels and visit the Incahuasi Island, home to towering cacti and panoramic views of the flats.

3. **Festivals and Cultural Experiences**: Bolivia's dry season is also packed with some of the country's most important cultural events. One highlight is La Paz's Gran Poder Festival in June, a lively celebration of traditional Bolivian dances, costumes, and music. In July, Fiesta de la Virgen del Carmen is celebrated across the country, particularly in the small town of Copacabana, where pilgrims gather to honor Bolivia's patron saint. If you're keen on witnessing Bolivia's vibrant traditions and rich cultural heritage, the dry season is an ideal time to visit.

**Wet Season (November to April)**: Though the wet season might seem less appealing due to frequent rains, it can offer a unique perspective on Bolivia's landscapes, transforming the country into a vibrant, green paradise. The wet season has its own charm and provides opportunities to see Bolivia in a completely different light.

1. **Salar de Uyuni's Mirror Effect**: One of the most magical sights in Bolivia occurs during the wet season, when rainwater collects on the surface of the Salar de Uyuni, creating a vast, natural mirror. This reflective surface perfectly captures the sky, creating surreal images where it's difficult to tell where the land ends and the sky begins. Photographers and adventurers alike flock to the salt flats during this time to experience this breathtaking phenomenon. If your dream is to see the salt flats' mirror effect, visiting between January and March will give you the best chances.

2. **The Amazon and Madidi National Park**: While the rainy season makes the Amazon Basin more humid and difficult to navigate, it also brings the jungle to life. Rivers swell, forests become lush and green, and wildlife activity increases. In Madidi National Park, one of the most biodiverse places on Earth, the wet season is a time of renewal. Although some trails may be muddy, this is when the Amazon is at its most vibrant, with abundant birdlife, butterflies, and flowering plants. For nature lovers, the wet season offers a unique opportunity to experience the jungle at its fullest.

3. **Fewer Tourists, More Authentic Experiences**: Another benefit of visiting during the wet season is the relative lack of tourists. While many travelers

avoid Bolivia during these months, those who do visit are rewarded with quieter attractions and more intimate experiences. Whether you're wandering through the colonial streets of Sucre or exploring the ruins of Tiwanaku, you'll likely have many of these places almost to yourself. This can provide a more authentic, unhurried experience of Bolivia, allowing you to connect more deeply with the local culture and landscapes.

**Regional Variations in Climate:** While the distinction between wet and dry seasons is a general guide, Bolivia's diverse geography means that different regions experience their own microclimates.

1. **The Altiplano (La Paz, Potosí, Salar de Uyuni):** The Altiplano, which includes popular destinations like La Paz, Potosí, and the Salar de Uyuni, is typically cooler year-round due to its high elevation. Temperatures during the dry season can drop significantly at night, especially in places like Uyuni and Potosí, so be sure to pack warm clothing. The wet season brings more moderate temperatures, but also the possibility of rain, particularly in January and February.

2. **The Amazon Basin (Rurrenabaque, Madidi National Park):** The lowland regions of the Amazon Basin are hot and humid throughout the year. In the dry season, temperatures can soar, while the wet season brings heavy rains and higher humidity. For jungle trekking and wildlife tours, the dry season (May to October) offers more comfortable conditions, but the wet season (November to April) is when the rainforest is at its most lush and alive.

3. **The Yungas (Coroico, Death Road):** The Yungas region, known for its subtropical valleys and the famous Death Road, lies between the Altiplano and the Amazon. This region can be visited year-round, but the wet season brings more frequent rain and mist, which can make the Death Road more challenging to traverse. In the dry season, the Yungas offer cooler, more pleasant temperatures for outdoor activities like biking and hiking.

## When to Visit Based on Your Interests

1. **Outdoor Adventure:** If you're planning on hiking, biking, or trekking through Bolivia's rugged landscapes, the dry season (May to October) is your best bet. The cooler, more stable weather makes it easier to explore places like La

Paz, Salar de Uyuni, and the Yungas. For high-altitude adventures, the dry season ensures safer trails and clearer skies.

2. **Wildlife and Nature Lovers:** For travelers looking to experience Bolivia's wildlife and lush landscapes, the wet season (November to April) is ideal. The Amazon Basin is alive with activity, and the Salar de Uyuni's mirror effect is a must-see. While some areas may be more difficult to access due to rain, the natural beauty of Bolivia during the wet season is undeniable.

3. **Cultural Festivals:** If you're keen on experiencing Bolivia's festivals and vibrant traditions, plan your visit around major events like the Gran Poder Festival (June), the Fiesta de la Virgen de la Candelaria (February), or the Oruro Carnival (February). These cultural celebrations are at the heart of Bolivian life and offer a deep dive into the country's rich heritage.

No matter when you visit, Bolivia promises adventure, beauty, and unforgettable experiences. Each season brings its own unique charm, whether it's the clear skies of the dry season or the vibrant landscapes of the wet season. By understanding Bolivia's climate and choosing the right time for your journey, you'll ensure that your trip is nothing short of extraordinary.

# TRAVEL ESSENTIALS

Bolivia is a country of vast contrasts, from the high-altitude plains of the Andes to the lush jungles of the Amazon Basin. With such diverse landscapes and a unique cultural heritage, traveling in Bolivia can be an adventure unlike any other. To ensure your trip is as smooth and enjoyable as possible, it's important to prepare well. Here's a comprehensive guide to the travel essentials you'll need to make the most of your Bolivian experience.

**Travel Documents and Visa Requirements:** Before embarking on your Bolivian adventure, it's essential to ensure that all your travel documents are in order. Bolivia has specific entry requirements depending on your nationality, so it's important to check what applies to you.

1. **Visas:** Citizens of many countries can visit Bolivia without a visa for stays of up to 90 days, including travelers from most European Union nations, the United States, Canada, Australia, and several others. However, it's always wise to double-check the latest visa requirements before your trip. If you're planning to stay longer, or if you're from a country that requires a visa, you'll need to apply in advance, either through a Bolivian embassy or consulate or via an online visa application system.

2. **Passport:** Your passport should be valid for at least six months beyond your planned departure date from Bolivia. Make sure it has enough blank pages for entry and exit stamps.

3. **Yellow Fever Vaccination:** While not always required, it is highly recommended to get a yellow fever vaccination if you're planning to visit Bolivia's tropical regions, especially the Amazon Basin and Madidi National Park. Some countries may even require proof of vaccination when traveling to Bolivia from areas where yellow fever is present.

4. **Travel Insurance:** Having comprehensive travel insurance is a must when visiting Bolivia. Ensure that your policy covers medical emergencies, trip cancellations, lost luggage, and, importantly, emergency evacuation, especially if you're heading into remote or high-altitude regions.

**Health and Safety Essentials:** When traveling to a destination as diverse and unique as Bolivia, your health and safety should always be a priority. Bolivia's geography and climate can pose certain challenges, particularly for those unaccustomed to high altitudes or tropical diseases. To ensure your well-being while exploring this beautiful country, be sure to pack the following health essentials:

1. **Altitude Sickness Medication:** Bolivia is famous for its high-altitude destinations, such as La Paz, which sits at an altitude of 3,650 meters (11,975 feet) above sea level, and Potosí, which is even higher. The combination of thin air, lower oxygen levels, and rapid altitude changes can lead to altitude sickness, also known as acute mountain sickness (AMS). Symptoms can include headaches, nausea, dizziness, and fatigue. To avoid AMS, it's recommended to acclimatize gradually and stay hydrated. Diamox (acetazolamide) is commonly prescribed to help with altitude sickness, but you should consult with your doctor before your trip to discuss medications that may work best for you.

2. **Vaccinations:** Before your trip to Bolivia, consult with a healthcare professional regarding any recommended vaccinations. The CDC and World Health Organization suggest that travelers consider vaccinations for hepatitis A, hepatitis B, typhoid, diphtheria, tetanus, and cholera. For those traveling to the Amazon or lowland areas, a malaria prophylaxis may be recommended.

3. **Insect Repellent and Mosquito Protection:** In Bolivia's lowland areas, including the Amazon and Madidi National Park, mosquitoes can carry diseases such as dengue, malaria, and Zika virus. Be sure to pack an effective insect repellent containing DEET, picaridin, or oil of lemon eucalyptus to protect yourself from bites. Wearing long sleeves and pants, especially during dawn and dusk, can further reduce your exposure to mosquitoes.

4. **Water Purification:** In Bolivia, tap water is generally not safe to drink. Always drink bottled water or use a water purification system, such as iodine tablets or a portable water filter, to make sure you're consuming clean water. This is especially important if you're traveling in more remote regions or during excursions.

5. **First Aid Kit**: Pack a basic first aid kit with essential items such as band-aids, antiseptic wipes, painkillers, cold medicine, and any prescription medications you may need. It's also wise to include things like electrolyte packets, which are helpful for hydration at high altitudes.

**Packing List for Bolivia**: What you pack for Bolivia depends on the time of year you're visiting and which regions you'll be exploring, as the country offers vastly different climates in different areas. Here's a comprehensive packing list to help you prepare for your Bolivian adventure.

Clothing:

- **Light, breathable clothing**: If you're heading to the Amazon Basin, pack light, moisture-wicking clothes for the hot and humid climate. Choose long-sleeve shirts and pants to protect yourself from mosquitoes and sun exposure.

- **Warm layers**: Bolivia's high-altitude regions can be cold, especially in the evenings and at night. Even in the dry season, temperatures can drop significantly. Be sure to pack warm layers, including a jacket, fleece, and gloves for the Altiplano, where temperatures can dip below freezing.

- **Sun protection**: With the high altitude and strong sun, it's essential to protect yourself from UV rays. Pack a wide-brimmed hat, sunglasses, sunscreen, and lip balm with SPF to avoid sunburns.

- **Sturdy hiking boots**: Bolivia offers many opportunities for trekking, from the Andean mountain ranges to the salt flats of Uyuni. A pair of sturdy, comfortable hiking boots is essential for exploring the country's rugged terrain.

- **Swimwear**: If you're visiting Lake Titicaca or enjoying the amenities of a hotel with a pool, don't forget to pack swimwear.

Electronics:

- **Universal power adapter**: Bolivia uses the A and C type plugs, so make sure you bring a universal power adapter to charge your electronics. The standard voltage is 230V, so be sure your devices are compatible.

- **Camera and extra memory cards**: Bolivia's landscapes and cultural sights are incredibly photogenic, so be sure to pack a camera, extra memory cards, and batteries.

- **Power bank**: Power outages can occasionally occur in Bolivia, especially in remote regions, so it's a good idea to bring a portable power bank to keep your devices charged on the go.

## Money and Currency:

- **Bolivian Boliviano (BOB)**: The currency used in Bolivia is the Bolivian boliviano (BOB). While ATMs are available in major cities like La Paz and Santa Cruz, it's advisable to carry cash, especially when traveling to rural areas. Be sure to carry smaller bills, as smaller shops and vendors may not accept larger denominations.

- **Credit cards**: Major credit cards are accepted at larger hotels and restaurants in Bolivia's main cities, but in smaller towns and rural areas, cash is the preferred method of payment. Always have cash on hand for smaller purchases, such as street food, transportation, and souvenirs.

## Travel Accessories:

- **Daypack**: A lightweight daypack is ideal for day trips, hikes, and excursions. It's perfect for carrying essentials like water, snacks, sunscreen, and a camera.

- **Water bottle**: Stay hydrated, especially in Bolivia's high-altitude regions, where the air can be dry and thin. Bring a reusable water bottle, which can help you save money and reduce plastic waste.

- **Guidebook and maps**: While mobile phones and GPS apps are useful, having a good old-fashioned guidebook or map can be handy, especially in remote areas with limited internet access.

**Safety and Security Tips**: Bolivia is generally a safe destination for travelers, but, as with any country, it's essential to stay vigilant and take precautions. Here are a few safety tips to ensure your trip goes smoothly:

1. **Avoiding Altitude Sickness:** Altitude sickness is one of the most common issues in Bolivia, especially for travelers arriving directly in La Paz or the Altiplano. Be sure to take it easy on your first day in high-altitude areas, drink plenty of water, and avoid strenuous activities until your body adjusts. Some travelers choose to take Diamox to help prevent altitude sickness, but always consult with a doctor before using any medication.

2. **Stay Alert in Crowded Areas:** Like in many parts of the world, pickpocketing can be a concern in crowded areas, especially in La Paz's busy markets or on public transport. Keep your valuables, such as your wallet and passport, in a secure location, and always be aware of your surroundings.

3. **Emergency Contacts:** In case of an emergency, it's helpful to know the local emergency numbers in Bolivia. **911** is the general emergency number, but you can also contact the nearest embassy for assistance in case of lost documents or other travel-related issues.

Bolivia offers an incredible range of experiences, from the salt flats of Uyuni to the vibrant cultural heritage of cities like Sucre and La Paz. By preparing with the right travel essentials, including the correct documents, clothing, health precautions, and safety measures, you'll be ready to embark on an unforgettable journey through one of South America's most fascinating countries.

# CHAPTER ONE
# PLANNING YOUR JOURNEY

Embarking on a journey to Bolivia is an adventure filled with breathtaking landscapes, rich cultural heritage, and vibrant cities. Before you set off, careful planning is essential to ensure a smooth and enriching experience. From the towering peaks of the Andes to the lush Amazon

rainforest, Bolivia offers a diverse range of attractions that cater to every traveler's interests. Begin by considering the best time to visit, which varies depending on the region and the activities you wish to pursue. Understanding the local climate, as well as potential festivals and events, can help you make the most of your trip.

Additionally, familiarizing yourself with Bolivia's unique travel requirements is crucial for a hassle-free experience. This includes securing the necessary visas, understanding health and safety precautions, and organizing transportation options within the country. Whether you prefer to explore bustling cities like La Paz and Sucre or venture into the natural wonders of Salar de Uyuni and Lake Titicaca, having a well-thought-out itinerary will allow you to savor the richness of Bolivian culture while creating unforgettable memories along the way.

# VISA AND ENTRY REQUIREMENTS

Traveling to Bolivia requires understanding the visa and entry requirements that apply to your nationality and the duration of your stay. Bolivia offers a variety of visa options, and knowing which one you need is crucial for a smooth arrival. Here are the key points to consider:

## Visa Types and Requirements

- **Tourist Visa:** Many nationalities, including those from the United States, Canada, the European Union, and several other countries, can enter Bolivia without a visa for short stays, typically up to 90 days. However, it's essential to check your specific country's requirements, as some may need to apply for a visa in advance. If you plan to stay longer or engage in activities like work or study, you may need to apply for a different type of visa.

- **Visa on Arrival:** For some travelers, Bolivia offers a visa-on-arrival option. This allows visitors to obtain a tourist visa upon entry at certain international airports. It usually requires presenting a valid passport, a return ticket, and proof of sufficient funds for your stay. The visa is typically valid for up to 90 days, and travelers may need to pay a fee in cash.

- **Electronic Visa (E-Visa):** Bolivia has implemented an electronic visa system for specific nationalities, allowing applicants to complete the visa application process online before their trip. This convenient option simplifies entry into the country and is ideal for travelers looking to secure their visa in advance.

**Passport Validity and Requirements:** Regardless of your visa type, your passport must be valid for at least six months beyond your planned departure date from Bolivia. Additionally, you should have at least one blank page for the entry stamp. It's advisable to carry a photocopy of your passport and visa with you during your travels, as authorities may require identification at various points.

**Health and Safety Considerations:** Before traveling, consider any health recommendations or vaccinations needed for entry into Bolivia. The country may have specific health regulations, especially concerning yellow fever vaccination for those coming from areas where the disease is present. Carrying proof of vaccinations might be necessary, so it's essential to consult with a healthcare provider or travel clinic well before your departure.

**Customs Regulations:** Upon entry, travelers must declare any items that could be subject to customs restrictions. This includes cash over a certain amount, agricultural products, and other goods. Familiarize yourself with the customs regulations to avoid any issues upon arrival. Additionally, it's advisable to keep receipts for any significant purchases or valuable items in case you need to declare them when leaving the country.

**Immigration Procedures:** Upon arrival, you will go through immigration control, where officials will check your visa (if required) and passport. Be prepared to answer questions about the purpose of your visit, your travel itinerary, and where you will be staying. Having a printed itinerary and accommodation details can expedite the process.

By understanding these visa and entry requirements, you can ensure that your journey to Bolivia starts on the right foot, allowing you to focus on exploring the breathtaking beauty and rich culture that awaits you.

# HEALTH AND SAFETY TIPS

Traveling to Bolivia presents a wealth of exciting experiences, but it's essential to prioritize your health and safety while exploring this diverse country. From navigating high-altitude locations to understanding local health considerations, these tips will help ensure a safe and enjoyable journey.

**Altitude Sickness Awareness:** One of the most significant health concerns when traveling to Bolivia is altitude sickness, especially if you plan to visit cities like La Paz, which is located at about 3,650 meters (11,975 feet) above sea level. Symptoms can include headaches, nausea, dizziness, and fatigue. To mitigate the risk of altitude sickness, consider the following:

- **Acclimatization:** If possible, spend a few days at lower altitudes (like Cochabamba) before ascending to higher elevations. This gradual acclimatization allows your body to adjust to the decrease in oxygen levels.

- **Hydration:** Drink plenty of water to stay hydrated, as the dry air and high altitude can lead to dehydration. Avoid alcohol and caffeine, as they can exacerbate dehydration and increase the risk of altitude sickness.

- **Medications:** Over-the-counter medications like acetazolamide (Diamox) can help prevent altitude sickness. Consult with a healthcare professional before your trip to see if this is a suitable option for you.

**Vaccinations and Health Precautions:** Before traveling to Bolivia, it's important to ensure that you are up-to-date on routine vaccines as well as any recommended travel vaccinations. Common vaccines to consider include:

- **Hepatitis A and B:** These vaccines are recommended due to the risk of transmission through contaminated food or water.

- **Typhoid:** This vaccine is advisable, particularly if you plan to eat street food or stay with locals.

- **Yellow Fever:** A vaccination is required if you are traveling from a country where yellow fever is present. The vaccination must be administered at least ten days before your arrival in Bolivia.

- **Rabies:** If you plan to engage in activities that might put you at risk (like hiking in rural areas or interacting with animals), consider getting vaccinated against rabies.

**Food and Water Safety:** Bolivia offers a vibrant culinary scene, but food safety should be a priority to avoid gastrointestinal illnesses:

- **Drink Bottled Water:** Tap water is not safe to drink in most parts of Bolivia. Always opt for bottled water, and check that the seal is intact before purchasing.

- **Be Cautious with Street Food:** While street food can be delicious and a part of the local experience, be selective about where you eat. Choose vendors that appear clean and have a high turnover of food.

- **Eat Fully Cooked Foods:** Ensure that the food you consume is cooked thoroughly and served hot. Raw fruits and vegetables should be washed with safe water or peeled to avoid contamination.

**Personal Safety Precautions:** While Bolivia is generally safe for tourists, exercising caution is advisable:

- **Stay Aware of Your Surroundings:** Be vigilant in crowded places, and keep an eye on your belongings. Pickpocketing can occur in tourist areas and public transportation.

- **Use Reputable Transportation:** When moving around cities, use established transportation options, such as registered taxis or ride-sharing services, rather than accepting rides from strangers.

- **Travel in Groups:** Whenever possible, travel with others, especially at night. This enhances your safety and allows for shared experiences.

**Emergency Contacts and Health Services:** Familiarize yourself with local emergency services before your trip. Make a note of emergency numbers (like police and ambulance services) and the location of the nearest hospital or clinic in the areas you plan to visit. Having travel insurance that covers health emergencies is highly recommended, as it can provide access to quality medical care.

Sun Protection and Insect Repellent: Given Bolivia's varied climates, sun protection is crucial:

- Sunscreen: Apply a broad-spectrum sunscreen with high SPF, especially at high altitudes where UV exposure increases.

- Insect Repellent: In areas like the Amazon, use insect repellent to protect against mosquito-borne illnesses such as dengue fever and Zika virus. Wear long sleeves and pants, particularly during dawn and dusk when mosquitoes are most active.

By taking these health and safety precautions into account, you can enjoy your Bolivian adventure with peace of mind, allowing you to focus on the breathtaking landscapes and rich cultural experiences that await you.

LA PAZ

# MONEY AND BUDGETING

Traveling to Bolivia can be an incredible adventure, but understanding the financial aspects is crucial for managing your budget effectively. From the local currency to budgeting tips, this section will guide you on how to handle your finances while enjoying all that Bolivia has to offer.

**Local Currency:** Bolivia's official currency is the Boliviano (BOB). As of now, the exchange rate fluctuates, so it's advisable to check the current rate before your trip. When traveling to Bolivia, consider the following tips regarding currency:

- **Currency Exchange:** You can exchange your currency at banks, official exchange offices, or ATMs in major cities. It's best to avoid exchanging money at hotels or street vendors, as the rates may not be favorable.

- **ATMs:** ATMs are widely available in urban areas, and they usually offer competitive exchange rates. However, not all ATMs accept international cards, so look for those that display logos of major networks like Visa or MasterCard. Keep in mind that there may be withdrawal limits, and fees can vary by bank.

- **Cash vs. Cards:** While credit and debit cards are accepted at larger establishments and some tourist attractions, cash is king in Bolivia. Many local markets, street vendors, and smaller restaurants only accept cash, so it's essential to carry enough bolivianos for day-to-day expenses.

**Budgeting for Your Trip:** Creating a budget before your trip will help you manage your finances effectively and enjoy your travel experience without stress. Here's how to approach budgeting for your journey:

- **Daily Expenses:** On average, travelers can expect to spend between $30 to $70 per day, depending on their travel style. This estimate typically includes accommodation, meals, transportation, and activities. Backpackers may find ways to travel on a tighter budget, while those seeking more comfort might spend significantly more.

- **Accommodation Costs:** Bolivia offers a range of accommodation options, from budget hostels and guesthouses to mid-range hotels and luxury stays. Expect to pay around $10 to $25 per night for budget accommodations, $30 to $70 for mid-range hotels, and upwards of $100 for luxury options, especially in popular tourist areas.

- **Food and Dining:** Dining in Bolivia is relatively affordable. Meals at local restaurants can range from $2 to $10, while dining at upscale establishments may cost $15 or more per person. Street food offers delicious and inexpensive options, allowing you to sample local flavors without breaking the bank.

- **Transportation Expenses:** Public transportation in Bolivia, including buses and shared taxis, is inexpensive. A long-distance bus ride between major cities may cost between $10 and $30. For local travel, expect to pay around $0.50 to $2 for short bus rides or shared taxis. Renting a bicycle or using ride-sharing apps can also be economical and convenient.

**Managing Your Budget:** Once you have an estimate of your daily expenses, consider these tips for effective budget management while traveling:

- **Keep Track of Your Spending:** Use budgeting apps or maintain a simple notebook to record your daily expenses. This will help you stay aware of your spending habits and adjust as needed.

- **Set a Daily Limit:** Determine a daily spending limit based on your overall budget. This will encourage you to prioritize your expenses and make informed decisions about where to splurge or save.

- **Be Flexible:** While having a budget is essential, allow yourself some flexibility for unexpected experiences, such as spontaneous excursions or dining at a highly recommended restaurant. Consider setting aside a portion of your budget for these moments.

**Safety and Security of Your Money:** Protecting your money while traveling is paramount. Here are some tips to ensure your finances remain secure:

- **Carry Multiple Forms of Payment:** Avoid relying solely on cash or a single credit card. Carry a mix of cash and at least one backup card stored separately from your primary card. This way, if one method is lost or stolen, you will have alternatives.

- **Use a Money Belt:** Consider using a money belt or hidden pouch to store your cash, cards, and important documents securely. Keep only small amounts of cash accessible for daily expenses.

- **Notify Your Bank:** Inform your bank of your travel plans to avoid having your card blocked due to suspicious activity. This will ensure you can access your funds without any interruptions.

By understanding Bolivia's currency and implementing effective budgeting strategies, you can enjoy your trip without financial worries. With careful planning, you'll be able to explore the country's rich culture, stunning landscapes, and unforgettable experiences while managing your money wisely.

Traveling to Bolivia can be an incredible adventure, but understanding the financial aspects is crucial for managing your budget effectively. From the local currency to budgeting tips, this section will guide you on how to handle your finances while enjoying all that Bolivia has to offer.

**Local Currency:** Bolivia's official currency is the Boliviano (BOB). As of now, the exchange rate fluctuates, so it's advisable to check the current rate before your trip. When traveling to Bolivia, consider the following tips regarding currency:

- **Currency Exchange:** You can exchange your currency at banks, official exchange offices, or ATMs in major cities. It's best to avoid exchanging money at hotels or street vendors, as the rates may not be favorable.

- **ATMs:** ATMs are widely available in urban areas, and they usually offer competitive exchange rates. However, not all ATMs accept international cards, so look for those that display logos of major networks like Visa or MasterCard. Keep in mind that there may be withdrawal limits, and fees can vary by bank.

- **Cash vs. Cards:** While credit and debit cards are accepted at larger establishments and some tourist attractions, cash is king in Bolivia. Many local markets, street vendors, and smaller restaurants only accept cash, so it's essential to carry enough bolivianos for day-to-day expenses.

**Budgeting for Your Trip:** Creating a budget before your trip will help you manage your finances effectively and enjoy your travel experience without stress. Here's how to approach budgeting for your journey:

- **Daily Expenses:** On average, travelers can expect to spend between $30 to $70 per day, depending on their travel style. This estimate typically includes accommodation, meals, transportation, and activities. Backpackers may find ways to travel on a tighter budget, while those seeking more comfort might spend significantly more.

- **Accommodation Costs:** Bolivia offers a range of accommodation options, from budget hostels and guesthouses to mid-range hotels and luxury stays. Expect to pay around $10 to $25 per night for budget accommodations, $30 to $70 for mid-range hotels, and upwards of $100 for luxury options, especially in popular tourist areas.

- **Food and Dining:** Dining in Bolivia is relatively affordable. Meals at local restaurants can range from $2 to $10, while dining at upscale establishments may cost $15 or more per person. Street food offers delicious and inexpensive options, allowing you to sample local flavors without breaking the bank.

- **Transportation Expenses:** Public transportation in Bolivia, including buses and shared taxis, is inexpensive. A long-distance bus ride between major cities may cost between $10 and $30. For local travel, expect to pay around $0.50 to $2 for short bus rides or shared taxis. Renting a bicycle or using ride-sharing apps can also be economical and convenient.

**Managing Your Budget:** Once you have an estimate of your daily expenses, consider these tips for effective budget management while traveling:

- **Keep Track of Your Spending:** Use budgeting apps or maintain a simple notebook to record your daily expenses. This will help you stay aware of your spending habits and adjust as needed.

- **Set a Daily Limit:** Determine a daily spending limit based on your overall budget. This will encourage you to prioritize your expenses and make informed decisions about where to splurge or save.

- **Be Flexible:** While having a budget is essential, allow yourself some flexibility for unexpected experiences, such as spontaneous excursions or dining at a highly recommended restaurant. Consider setting aside a portion of your budget for these moments.

**Safety and Security of Your Money:** Protecting your money while traveling is paramount. Here are some tips to ensure your finances remain secure:

- **Carry Multiple Forms of Payment:** Avoid relying solely on cash or a single credit card. Carry a mix of cash and at least one backup card stored separately from your primary card. This way, if one method is lost or stolen, you will have alternatives.

- **Use a Money Belt:** Consider using a money belt or hidden pouch to store your cash, cards, and important documents securely. Keep only small amounts of cash accessible for daily expenses.

- **Notify Your Bank:** Inform your bank of your travel plans to avoid having your card blocked due to suspicious activity. This will ensure you can access your funds without any interruptions.

By understanding Bolivia's currency and implementing effective budgeting strategies, you can enjoy your trip without financial worries. With careful planning, you'll be able to explore the country's rich culture, stunning landscapes, and unforgettable experiences while managing your money wisely.

# CHAPTER TWO
# WHERE TO STAY

Finding the right accommodation in Bolivia is essential for maximizing your travel experience, whether you're seeking luxury, comfort, or budget-friendly options. The country offers a diverse range of lodging choices, from high-end

hotels in bustling cities like La Paz to charming hostels in the serene landscapes of the Andes. Each region provides unique accommodations that reflect the local culture and hospitality, ensuring that you have a place to recharge after a day of exploration. Researching your options based on location, amenities, and price can help you secure the perfect spot for your stay, enhancing your overall journey.

When planning your accommodation, consider the various neighborhoods that suit your travel style. In La Paz, the historic center offers easy access to attractions, while areas like Sopocachi and Miraflores provide a more relaxed atmosphere with excellent dining and nightlife options. If you're heading to the Amazon Basin, eco-lodges and jungle resorts offer an immersive experience in nature. Meanwhile, destinations like Uyuni, known for its stunning salt flats, have a variety of guesthouses that cater to different budgets. Regardless of your choice, Bolivia's rich tapestry of accommodation options will make your stay comfortable and memorable, allowing you to immerse yourself fully in the country's vibrant culture and breathtaking landscapes.

# LUXURY ACCOMMODATIONS

Bolivia may not be the first country that comes to mind when you think of luxury travel, but it offers a selection of upscale accommodations that combine comfort, style, and unique local experiences. Whether you're looking for opulent hotels in bustling cities or serene retreats surrounded by nature, Bolivia has luxurious options that cater to discerning travelers seeking exceptional service and unforgettable stays.

**Urban Luxury in La Paz:** La Paz, the highest capital city in the world, boasts several luxurious hotels that provide stunning views of the Andes and the cityscape. Here are some top choices:

- **Hotel Ritz Lago Titicaca:** Located on the shores of Lake Titicaca, this hotel features elegantly designed rooms with panoramic views, combining traditional Bolivian decor with modern amenities. Guests can enjoy fine dining options, a wellness spa, and easy access to boat trips on the lake. The peaceful ambiance and exceptional service make it an ideal base for exploring this majestic region.

- **Casa Grande Hotel:** Situated in the upscale neighborhood of La Paz, Casa Grande Hotel is known for its luxurious accommodations and personalized service. The hotel features spacious rooms with contemporary design, a full-service spa, and a rooftop pool offering breathtaking views of the city. The on-site restaurant serves a diverse menu, showcasing both Bolivian and international cuisine, ensuring that guests have a memorable dining experience.

- Hotel Europa: This five-star hotel combines elegance with a touch of Bolivian culture. Its rooms are beautifully appointed with luxurious furnishings and modern amenities. Hotel Europa also offers a gourmet restaurant, a stylish bar, and a well-equipped gym, making it a great choice for both leisure and business travelers.

**Unique Stays in Uyuni:** Uyuni is famous for its mesmerizing salt flats, and several luxury accommodations here allow travelers to experience this breathtaking landscape in comfort:

- **Hotel Palacio de Sal:** Constructed entirely of salt, this unique hotel offers guests a one-of-a-kind experience. The hotel features spacious rooms with salt block walls and comfortable furnishings. Amenities include a spa, gourmet dining, and organized tours of the nearby Salar de Uyuni. Staying at Palacio de Sal is not just about luxury; it's an opportunity to immerse yourself in the surreal beauty of the salt flats.

- **Luna Salada Hotel:** Perched on the edge of the salt flats, Luna Salada Hotel provides an upscale experience with stunning views. The hotel boasts well-appointed rooms, a restaurant offering local cuisine, and a bar with panoramic views of the salt flats. Its location makes it an ideal launching point for exploring the surreal landscapes of the Salar de Uyuni.

**Nature-Inspired Luxury in the Amazon:** Bolivia's Amazon region also features luxurious eco-lodges that offer unique experiences while immersing guests in the lush jungle environment:

- **Bala Lodge:** Located in the heart of the Bolivian Amazon, Bala Lodge offers luxurious accommodations surrounded by pristine nature. The lodge features spacious, tastefully decorated bungalows with private balconies overlooking the river. Guests can enjoy guided excursions into the jungle, wildlife observation, and cultural experiences with local communities. With its commitment to sustainability and comfort, Bala Lodge provides a tranquil escape from the hustle and bustle of city life.

- **Copaibo Ecolodge:** Nestled in the Madidi National Park, Copaibo Ecolodge provides an exclusive experience for travelers seeking adventure and relaxation. The lodge features luxurious accommodations with an emphasis on eco-friendliness. Guests can explore the biodiversity of the surrounding rainforest, take part in guided treks, and enjoy gourmet meals made from locally sourced ingredients. The emphasis on sustainable tourism and luxury makes Copaibo an exceptional choice for nature lovers.

**High-End Amenities and Services:** Luxury accommodations in Bolivia not only offer stunning environments but also high-end amenities that enhance your stay. Many hotels provide:

- **Spa Services:** Many luxury hotels feature full-service spas offering a range of treatments, from massages to beauty therapies, allowing guests to unwind after a day of exploration.

- **Fine Dining:** Upscale accommodations typically include on-site restaurants that serve gourmet cuisine, often highlighting local ingredients and flavors. This allows guests to experience the culinary richness of Bolivia without venturing far from their hotels.

- **Personalized Services:** High-end hotels often provide personalized concierge services to assist guests in planning activities, making reservations, and providing insider tips about local attractions.

- **Exclusive Experiences:** Many luxury accommodations offer exclusive experiences such as private tours, cultural workshops, or adventure activities, ensuring a tailor-made travel experience that goes beyond the ordinary.

By choosing luxury accommodations in Bolivia, you can enjoy the country's rich culture and stunning landscapes while indulging in comfort and high-end amenities. Whether you're marveling at the salt flats, exploring the Amazon, or soaking in the vibrant city life, these luxurious options provide a perfect retreat for discerning travelers seeking the best of what Bolivia has to offer.

# BUDGET-FRIENDLY OPTIONS

Traveling in Bolivia doesn't have to break the bank. The country is filled with a variety of budget-friendly accommodations that offer comfort, convenience, and an authentic taste of local culture without the hefty price tag. Whether you're a backpacker, a student, or a traveler on a tight

budget, Bolivia provides plenty of options to ensure you can explore its rich landscapes and vibrant cities while keeping costs manageable.

**Hostels:** Hostels are one of the most popular choices for budget travelers in Bolivia, particularly in major cities like La Paz, Sucre, and Santa Cruz. They offer affordable rates, often starting from as low as $8 to $15 per night for dormitory-style accommodation. Here are some notable options:

- **The Adventure Brew Hostel (La Paz):** Known for its friendly atmosphere and lively social scene, The Adventure Brew Hostel offers both dorms and private rooms. Guests can enjoy a complimentary breakfast, a bar with house-brewed beer, and a communal kitchen. The hostel also organizes tours and activities, making it easy for travelers to meet others and share experiences.

- **Oso Hostel (Sucre):** Located in the heart of Sucre, Oso Hostel provides comfortable dormitory and private rooms at affordable prices. It features a cozy common area, a well-equipped kitchen, and a terrace with great views of the city. The friendly staff is always willing to help with travel tips and recommendations, making it an ideal base for exploring the beautiful colonial city.

- **Hostal Casa de La Gringa (Copacabana):** Situated near Lake Titicaca, this charming hostel offers both dorms and private rooms at budget-friendly prices. Guests can enjoy a relaxing garden area, a shared kitchen, and easy access to local attractions, including boat trips to Isla del Sol.

**Guesthouses and Homestays:** For those seeking a more local experience, guesthouses and homestays provide budget-friendly options that allow travelers to immerse themselves in Bolivian culture. These accommodations often feature simple but comfortable rooms, friendly hosts, and home-cooked meals.

- **Hostal La Cupula (La Paz):** This guesthouse is located on a hillside, offering stunning views of the city. It features clean and comfortable rooms, a shared kitchen, and a cozy atmosphere. Guests often rave about the delicious breakfast options and the friendly staff, who can provide insight into local attractions.

- **Casa de los Abuelos (Sucre):** A homely guesthouse that emphasizes a family-friendly atmosphere, Casa de los Abuelos offers basic but cozy accommodations. The hosts provide guests with local insights and delicious breakfast options, making it a favorite among travelers looking for an authentic experience in Sucre.

- **Hostal Figueroa (Potosí):** Located in the historical city of Potosí, this guesthouse offers comfortable rooms at reasonable prices. It's well-situated for exploring the city's rich history and colonial architecture, and the friendly owners are eager to share recommendations and assist with travel plans.

**Budget Hotels and Eco-Lodges:** Bolivia also has a range of budget hotels and eco-lodges that cater to those looking for a bit more comfort while keeping costs low. These options often provide essential amenities, making them ideal for longer stays.

- **Hotel Nido del Condor (La Paz):** A budget hotel that offers clean and comfortable rooms with basic amenities, Hotel Nido del Condor is conveniently located near public transport and local attractions. It features a cozy dining area where guests can enjoy breakfast, and the staff is known for their hospitality.

- **Eco Lodge La Cumbre (Coroico):** Set in the lush landscapes of Coroico, this eco-lodge offers affordable accommodations in a tranquil setting. Guests can enjoy the beautiful views, nature trails, and a relaxing atmosphere while having access to shared kitchen facilities. The lodge promotes sustainable practices, making it an ideal choice for eco-conscious travelers.

- **Hotel Santa Teresa (Sucre):** This budget-friendly hotel is located in the heart of Sucre and offers simple, clean rooms at competitive rates. With amenities like Wi-Fi, breakfast options, and a friendly atmosphere, it's a popular choice among travelers looking for comfort without the high price tag.

**Camping and Alternative Options:** For the more adventurous traveler, camping can be a thrilling and economical way to experience Bolivia's stunning landscapes. Some national parks and areas near Lake Titicaca offer camping facilities, where you can pitch your tent and enjoy the great outdoors.

- **Salar de Uyuni Camping:** Many tour operators in Uyuni offer camping trips on the salt flats, where travelers can spend a night under the stars, surrounded by the otherworldly beauty of the landscape. This unique experience often includes meals and transportation, making it a budget-friendly option for those looking to explore the flats in an unforgettable way.

- **Chacaltaya Mountain Camping:** For adventurous hikers, camping at high-altitude locations like Chacaltaya Mountain can be a thrilling experience. With breathtaking views of the surrounding Andes, this option allows you to connect with nature while enjoying Bolivia's stunning vistas.

## Tips for Saving Money on Accommodations

- **Book in Advance:** While some budget accommodations operate on a first-come, first-served basis, booking in advance, especially during peak travel seasons, can help you secure better rates and availability.

- **Consider Location:** Staying slightly outside of tourist hotspots can often lead to lower prices. Many budget-friendly options are available within a short walking distance or a cheap taxi ride from major attractions.

- **Look for Discounts:** Check for discounts or promotions through online booking platforms, or inquire directly with accommodations about any special offers for longer stays or group bookings.

By choosing budget-friendly accommodations in Bolivia, travelers can enjoy the country's rich culture and stunning landscapes without compromising comfort or breaking the bank. From hostels and guesthouses to eco-lodges and camping options, Bolivia provides a variety of affordable stays that cater to every traveler's needs, allowing for an enriching and memorable journey through this remarkable South American destination.

LAKE TITICACA

# UNIQUE AND ECO-FRIENDLY LODGING

Bolivia's commitment to sustainable tourism and preservation of its unique natural environments has given rise to a variety of eco-friendly and distinctive accommodations. These options not only provide an exceptional lodging experience but also allow travelers to enjoy the country's diverse landscapes while minimizing their environmental footprint. From eco-lodges nestled in the Amazon rainforest to luxury stays made from local materials, Bolivia offers a range of accommodations that cater to the growing demand for sustainable and eco-conscious travel.

**Eco-Lodges in the Amazon Rainforest:** The Bolivian Amazon is a haven for eco-tourism, and its eco-lodges allow visitors to experience the richness of the rainforest without compromising the ecosystem. These lodges are typically built with sustainable materials and offer an immersive experience in nature, promoting conservation efforts and community-based tourism.

- **Bala Lodge (Madidi National Park):** Nestled in one of the most biodiverse regions of the Amazon, Bala Lodge is a prime example of eco-tourism at its best. The lodge is committed to sustainability, with a focus on preserving the natural environment and promoting responsible tourism. The rooms are built using local materials and feature open-air designs that allow guests to connect with nature. Visitors can participate in guided wildlife walks, river excursions, and jungle treks, all while supporting local conservation initiatives. The lodge also emphasizes community development, offering employment opportunities to local indigenous groups.

- **Selva Bananito Lodge (Madidi National Park):** Located in the heart of Bolivia's Madidi National Park, this eco-lodge is a paradise for nature lovers. The lodge is built using natural materials like bamboo and thatch, and its design blends seamlessly with the surrounding rainforest. Guests can enjoy rustic yet comfortable accommodations while participating in wildlife observation, birdwatching tours, and guided hikes. The lodge also promotes sustainability by operating on solar energy and practicing waste reduction.

- **Refugio Los Volcanes (Pando):** Situated in the remote Pando region, Refugio Los Volcanes offers a unique and immersive eco-tourism experience. The lodge is dedicated to preserving the natural habitat of the surrounding rainforest and offers guided expeditions that focus on wildlife conservation. The lodge uses eco-friendly practices, such as rainwater harvesting, composting, and solar power, to minimize its environmental impact. Guests can enjoy the tranquility of the rainforest, observe rare species of animals and plants, and learn about sustainable practices from the lodge staff.

**Salar de Uyuni:** The Salar de Uyuni, one of Bolivia's most iconic natural landmarks, is home to some remarkable eco-friendly lodging options. Built from locally sourced materials and designed to minimize environmental impact, these accommodations allow guests to experience the breathtaking salt flats while supporting sustainable tourism practices.

- **Hotel Palacio de Sal (Uyuni):** A unique example of sustainable architecture, Hotel Palacio de Sal is constructed entirely of salt blocks, giving it a distinctive and surreal appearance. The hotel blends seamlessly with the surrounding landscape and offers comfortable, eco-conscious accommodations. Guests can enjoy a range of activities, including tours of the salt flats, stargazing, and exploring the local culture. The hotel promotes sustainability by using energy-efficient lighting, water-saving systems, and providing organic food options sourced from local farmers.

- **Luna Salada Hotel (Uyuni):** Perched on the edge of the Salar de Uyuni, Luna Salada Hotel offers guests a serene and eco-friendly retreat with stunning views of the salt flats. The hotel is built using salt and stone, with designs that reflect the region's natural beauty. It also operates sustainably, with a focus on reducing waste and conserving water and energy. The hotel offers guests the chance to experience the unique salt flats in comfort, with activities such as guided tours, bike rides, and visits to nearby towns.

**Community-Based Eco-Lodging:** Community-based eco-lodging options are becoming increasingly popular in Bolivia as a way to support local communities while promoting sustainable travel. These accommodations are often managed by indigenous communities and provide a deep connection to the culture and traditions of the region, all while minimizing their environmental impact.

- **Kara-ñavi Eco-Lodge (Yungas):** Located in the Yungas region, Kara-ñavi Eco-Lodge is an excellent example of community-based eco-tourism. The lodge is run by the local indigenous community, who are committed to preserving the environment while offering visitors an authentic experience of their culture. The lodge uses sustainable building practices, such as constructing cabins from local wood and using solar energy. Guests can enjoy activities such as hiking, birdwatching, and visiting local farms, all while supporting community-led conservation projects.

- **Ecolodge Laguna Colorada (Potosí):** Situated in the Eduardo Avaroa National Reserve, Ecolodge Laguna Colorada offers visitors the chance to stay in one of Bolivia's most stunning natural settings. The lodge is built using eco-friendly materials and focuses on sustainable tourism by employing local people and supporting conservation efforts in the region. The eco-lodge is an excellent base for exploring the surrounding landscape, including the otherworldly red lagoon, home to flamingos and other wildlife. The eco-lodge offers a range of activities, including birdwatching, trekking, and exploring nearby geysers.

**Sustainable Stays in the Andes:** The Andean highlands are home to a number of eco-friendly accommodations that combine comfort, sustainability, and stunning views. Many of these accommodations are built with traditional materials and design principles, offering guests a chance to experience Bolivia's culture while minimizing their environmental impact.

- **Eco-Inn (La Paz):** Located in the heart of La Paz, Eco-Inn is a boutique eco-hotel that uses green technologies, such as solar panels and energy-efficient lighting. The hotel is committed to sustainability, with a focus on waste reduction, water conservation, and supporting local producers. Guests can enjoy comfortable rooms with views of the city and mountains, as well as dine in an on-site restaurant that serves organic, locally sourced food.

- **Jardín de Los Andes (La Paz):** This eco-hotel is set amidst the spectacular Andean landscape, providing a peaceful retreat that combines luxury with sustainability. The hotel features eco-friendly practices such as rainwater harvesting, waste recycling, and organic gardening. The rooms are designed with traditional Andean decor and offer stunning views of the surrounding mountains. Guests can participate in eco-tours, visit nearby indigenous communities, and explore the natural beauty of the region.

**Solar-Powered Lodging:** For travelers seeking a unique experience that combines sustainability and innovation, Bolivia also offers solar-powered lodging options. These accommodations rely on renewable energy sources to minimize their environmental impact, making them a great choice for eco-conscious travelers.

- **Solar Lodge (Tupiza):** Located in the southern Bolivian town of Tupiza, Solar Lodge is an off-the-grid, solar-powered eco-lodge that provides an intimate and sustainable stay. The lodge uses solar panels for electricity and offers guests a chance to enjoy the region's dramatic landscapes while reducing their carbon footprint. Activities include guided treks through the desert and nearby canyons, horseback riding, and cultural tours.

- **Hostal Solar (Oruro):** Hostal Solar in Oruro is another excellent example of eco-friendly lodging in Bolivia. The hotel is entirely solar-powered and focuses on sustainability through energy efficiency, water conservation, and eco-friendly construction. Guests can enjoy comfortable rooms, an on-site restaurant that serves organic meals, and easy access to the city's cultural landmarks.

**Eco-Friendly Lodging Practices Across Bolivia:** In addition to specific eco-lodges and hotels, Bolivia as a whole has embraced sustainable tourism practices. Many accommodations, regardless of their size or location, are increasingly adopting eco-friendly practices such as:

- **Waste Reduction:** Many hotels and lodges in Bolivia have implemented systems to reduce waste, such as composting, recycling, and encouraging guests to use reusable water bottles and reduce plastic consumption.

- **Water and Energy Conservation:** Bolivia's eco-friendly accommodations often feature water-saving devices, energy-efficient lighting, and the use of solar energy to reduce their carbon footprint.

- **Local Sourcing:** Many accommodations in Bolivia prioritize sourcing food and materials locally, supporting Bolivian artisans, and reducing the environmental impact of transporting goods.

Bolivia's unique and eco-friendly lodging options provide travelers with a chance to explore its diverse landscapes while supporting conservation efforts and local communities. Whether you're staying in an eco-lodge in the Amazon rainforest, a solar-powered hotel in the desert, or a community-run guesthouse in the Andes, these accommodations ensure that your visit to Bolivia will be sustainable, memorable, and respectful of the natural beauty that the country has to offer.

LA PAZ CITY

# CHAPTER THREE
# LA PAZ AND SURROUNDINGS

Nestled high in the Andes Mountains, La Paz is a vibrant city that beautifully blends modernity with rich cultural heritage. As the highest capital in the world, its breathtaking elevation offers a unique vantage point to explore a city that pulsates with life. From the bustling markets of El Alto to the historic streets of the city center, La Paz invites travelers to immerse themselves in its dynamic atmosphere. Iconic landmarks such as the Witches' Market, where locals sell traditional potions and herbs, reflect the city's deep-rooted indigenous traditions, while contemporary attractions like the Valle de la Luna showcase Bolivia's stunning natural beauty. Visitors can also enjoy panoramic views of the snow-capped Illimani Mountain, providing a stunning backdrop to this fascinating urban landscape.

Beyond the city, the surrounding areas of La Paz offer a wealth of natural wonders and cultural experiences waiting to be discovered. Just a short drive away lies the picturesque town of Copacabana, perched on the shores of Lake Titicaca, where travelers can explore its serene waters and vibrant local culture. The nearby Moon Valley presents a surreal landscape of eroded rock formations that feels otherworldly. Outdoor enthusiasts can venture to the nearby Yungas, a lush region of cloud forests teeming with biodiversity, or hike to the ancient ruins of Tiwanaku, an archaeological site that sheds light on the region's pre-Columbian history. La Paz and its surroundings provide an incredible blend of urban exploration and natural adventure, making it a must-visit destination for any traveler seeking to experience the heart of Bolivia.

# TOP ATTRACTIONS IN LA PAZ

La Paz is a city brimming with cultural, historical, and natural attractions that capture the essence of Bolivia. Its unique setting in the Andes, combined with a rich tapestry of traditions and vibrant city life, makes it an unmissable destination. Here are some of the top attractions that showcase the beauty and diversity of La Paz:

1. **Plaza Murillo:** At the heart of La Paz, Plaza Murillo is the city's main square and serves as the epicenter of political and social life. Surrounded by important government buildings, including the Presidential Palace and the Cathedral of La Paz, the plaza is a hub of activity. Visitors can stroll through the square, admire the beautiful gardens and fountains, and witness local ceremonies and gatherings. The plaza is named after Pedro Domingo Murillo, a hero of Bolivia's struggle for independence. Nearby, the National Museum of Art offers a chance to delve into Bolivia's rich artistic heritage, showcasing works from pre-Columbian times to contemporary art.

2. **Valle de la Luna (Moon Valley):** Located just a short drive from the city center, Valle de la Luna is a striking geological formation that resembles a lunar landscape. The area features eroded rock formations, deep canyons, and unusual shapes created by years of wind and rain. Visitors can explore winding trails that provide stunning views of the unique landscape, making it a perfect spot for photography and leisurely walks. The surreal beauty of Valle de la Luna is enhanced by its proximity to La Paz, making it a popular excursion for both locals and tourists. The site is also home to several vendors selling handicrafts and snacks, allowing visitors to enjoy local flavors amidst the stunning scenery.

3. **Witches' Market (Mercado de las Brujas):** A visit to La Paz would not be complete without exploring the infamous Witches' Market, located in the heart of the city. This vibrant market is filled with stalls selling an array of traditional herbs, potions, amulets, and other items used in indigenous rituals. Visitors can witness local shamans and witch doctors performing rituals to bring luck, health, and prosperity to their clients. The atmosphere is colorful and lively, with the scent of various herbs and the sounds of bargaining filling the air. The Witches' Market offers a fascinating glimpse into the spiritual

beliefs and practices of Bolivian culture, making it an essential stop for those seeking to understand the country's unique traditions.

4. **San Francisco Church:** The San Francisco Church, an architectural masterpiece in the heart of La Paz, is one of the most significant colonial structures in the city. Built in the 18th century, the church showcases a blend of Baroque and indigenous architectural styles, evident in its intricately carved façade and stunning interior. The church is home to a rich collection of religious art, including paintings and sculptures, and is a site for various religious ceremonies and events. Visitors can explore the church and its adjoining convent, which provides insight into the historical and spiritual significance of the site. The vibrant square surrounding the church is also a great place to relax and enjoy the local atmosphere.

5. **Tiwanaku Archaeological Site:** A short trip from La Paz, the ancient ruins of Tiwanaku provide a fascinating glimpse into Bolivia's pre-Columbian history. Once a thriving civilization, Tiwanaku was a major cultural and political center over a thousand years ago. The site features impressive stone structures, including the iconic Gate of the Sun and the Akapana Pyramid, which highlight the architectural prowess of the Tiwanaku people. Guided tours are available to help visitors understand the historical context and significance of the ruins, as well as the various theories surrounding the civilization's decline. The nearby Tiwanaku Museum offers additional insights into the artifacts and history of this remarkable site.

6. **El Alto Market:** The bustling El Alto Market is one of the largest open-air markets in South America, located just outside of La Paz. This vibrant marketplace offers everything from clothing and handicrafts to electronics and fresh produce. A visit to El Alto provides a unique opportunity to experience daily life in Bolivia, as locals shop for goods and socialize with one another. The market is particularly famous for its wide selection of traditional foods, including salteñas (savory pastries) and anticuchos (grilled meat skewers). For those seeking an authentic Bolivian experience, a trip to El Alto Market is a must.

7. **Cholita Wrestling:** For an unforgettable cultural experience, attend a Cholita Wrestling event in La Paz. This unique form of entertainment features female

wrestlers, known as cholitas, who don traditional Aymara attire while engaging in humorous and often theatrical wrestling matches. The events are colorful and lively, combining elements of traditional Bolivian culture with modern wrestling theatrics. Spectators can cheer for their favorite cholita, enjoy local snacks, and revel in the joyous atmosphere. Cholita Wrestling provides a fantastic glimpse into the empowerment of women in Bolivian society while showcasing the country's vibrant culture.

8. **Killi Killi Viewpoint:** For panoramic views of La Paz and its breathtaking mountainous backdrop, head to the Killi Killi Viewpoint. Located on a hilltop, this scenic spot offers stunning vistas of the city's sprawling landscape, including the majestic Illimani mountain range. It's an ideal location for photographers and anyone wanting to take in the beauty of La Paz from above. The viewpoint is particularly popular at sunset, when the city lights begin to twinkle against the dusky sky, creating a magical atmosphere. A visit to Killi Killi is perfect for those seeking a moment of tranquility amidst the hustle and bustle of the city.

9. **Murillo Palace:** The Murillo Palace is the official residence of the President of Bolivia and serves as a symbol of the country's political history. Located near Plaza Murillo, this neoclassical building is open to the public during special events, providing a glimpse into the country's political life. The palace is adorned with beautiful artworks and historic artifacts, offering visitors insight into Bolivia's rich cultural heritage. Guided tours may be available, allowing guests to explore the ornate rooms and learn about the significance of the palace in Bolivian history.

10. **Cable Car System (Mi Teleférico):** One of the most innovative transportation systems in the world, the Mi Teleférico cable car system connects La Paz with El Alto and other surrounding areas. Riding the cable car offers a unique perspective of the city as it glides above the bustling streets and scenic landscapes. Each line provides stunning views of the Andes and the sprawling urban environment below. It's not just a means of transportation; it's an experience that showcases the engineering marvel of the city while offering a breathtaking bird's-eye view of La Paz.

La Paz is a city that captivates with its eclectic mix of history, culture, and stunning natural beauty. From exploring ancient ruins to immersing oneself in local traditions, the top attractions in La Paz offer something for every traveler, ensuring a memorable journey through one of South America's most unique cities.

TOWN OF COPACABANA

# CULTURAL EXPERIENCES

La Paz is not only Bolivia's administrative capital but also a vibrant cultural hub that encapsulates the essence of Bolivian identity, blending indigenous traditions with colonial influences. The city's rich cultural tapestry is woven through its festivals, art, music, and daily life, offering visitors a unique opportunity to engage with its diverse heritage. Here are some of the most enriching cultural experiences that La Paz has to offer:

**Traditional Festivals:** La Paz hosts a plethora of colorful festivals throughout the year, each reflecting the city's rich cultural heritage and indigenous traditions. One of the most prominent is La Fiesta de la Alasita, celebrated in January. This festival honors the Aymara god of abundance and is marked by the sale of miniature goods, symbolizing prosperity and success. Locals purchase tiny replicas of houses, cars, and money, which they later have blessed by priests. The festival culminates in a vibrant parade featuring traditional dances, music, and colorful costumes, showcasing the deep-rooted beliefs of the Aymara people.

Another significant celebration is El Gran Poder, held in June, which features a spectacular procession of dancers and musicians. Participants don elaborate costumes and perform traditional dances that represent various Bolivian cultures. The festival celebrates the patron saint of La Paz, Señor Jesús del Gran Poder, and is a lively display of faith, community spirit, and cultural pride. Attending these festivals allows visitors to witness the heart and soul of Bolivian culture in a truly immersive environment.

**Local Markets:** Exploring La Paz's bustling markets is a must for anyone wanting to experience the city's local culture. The Mercado de las Brujas (Witches' Market) offers a glimpse into the spiritual side of Bolivian life, where traditional herbal remedies, amulets, and spiritual artifacts are sold. Here, visitors can engage with local shamans, learn about indigenous healing practices, and purchase unique souvenirs. The vibrant atmosphere is filled with the sounds of bargaining and the enticing aromas of local foods.

Another noteworthy market is the Mercado Lanza, where you can find an array of fresh produce, textiles, and local delicacies. This market is frequented by locals and provides a true taste of everyday life in La Paz. Sampling traditional dishes such as salteñas (savory pastries) and anticuchos (grilled meat skewers) while mingling with the locals is an excellent way to engage with the community and understand their culinary culture.

**Art and Museums:** La Paz is home to a thriving arts scene that reflects its diverse cultural heritage. The Museo Nacional de Arte is a highlight, showcasing an extensive collection of Bolivian art, from colonial to contemporary works. Visitors can explore pieces by renowned artists and gain insight into Bolivia's artistic evolution. The museum often hosts temporary exhibitions and cultural events, making it a lively center for artistic expression.

For those interested in indigenous culture, the Museo de Etnografía y Folklore provides a comprehensive overview of Bolivia's various ethnic groups. The museum's exhibits feature traditional clothing, textiles, and artifacts that illustrate the rich history and customs of the country's indigenous peoples. Engaging with the exhibits allows visitors to appreciate the depth of Bolivia's cultural diversity and the importance of preserving these traditions.

**Music and Dance:** Music and dance are integral to Bolivian culture, and La Paz is the perfect place to experience this vibrant aspect of life. Traditional Aymara and Quechua music often features instruments such as the charango (a small stringed instrument), pan flutes, and drums, creating a distinctive sound that is both captivating and rhythmic. Numerous venues and cultural centers throughout the city host live music performances, offering a chance to enjoy local artists while soaking in the atmosphere.

One of the most iconic forms of dance is the Moreno, performed during festivals and celebrations. This lively dance symbolizes the merging of African and indigenous cultures and is characterized by intricate footwork and colorful costumes. Participating in or watching these performances provides a deeper understanding of Bolivia's cultural history and the stories that are expressed through movement and music.

**Culinary Workshops:** Bolivia's culinary landscape is as diverse as its culture, and participating in a cooking workshop is a delightful way to engage with the local gastronomy. Many local chefs offer hands-on classes that teach participants how to prepare traditional dishes using fresh, local ingredients. Learning to make salteñas, llajwa (a spicy salsa), or even the national dish, sajta de pollo (chicken in a spicy peanut sauce), allows visitors to connect with the culinary traditions of the country while enjoying a delicious meal.

These workshops often include a market tour, where participants can purchase ingredients and learn about their significance in Bolivian cooking. This immersive experience not only provides valuable cooking skills but also fosters a deeper appreciation for the flavors and cultural significance behind each dish.

**Community Engagement:** For a truly authentic cultural experience, visitors can participate in community projects or volunteer opportunities. Engaging with local organizations that focus on education, healthcare, or environmental initiatives provides a meaningful way to connect with the people of La Paz. Many organizations welcome short-term volunteers, allowing visitors to contribute to local communities while gaining insight into the daily lives and challenges faced by residents.

This kind of engagement fosters mutual understanding and respect, enabling visitors to leave La Paz with lasting memories and connections to the community. The experiences gained through community involvement can often be the highlight of a trip, offering a unique perspective on the culture and lifestyle of the Bolivian people.

La Paz is a city that pulsates with life and culture, offering visitors a myriad of experiences that delve deep into its history, traditions, and everyday life. From colorful festivals to engaging with local artisans and exploring the culinary landscape, there are countless ways to connect with the heart of Bolivian culture. By immersing yourself in these cultural experiences, you'll gain a deeper appreciation for La Paz and the vibrant heritage that makes it such a captivating destination.

MAIN SQUARE OF POTOSI

# DAY TRIPS FROM LA PAZ

La Paz is not only a vibrant city filled with culture and history but also serves as a perfect base for exploring some of Bolivia's most stunning natural landscapes and intriguing historical sites. From ancient ruins to breathtaking natural wonders, there are plenty of day trip options that will allow you to experience the rich diversity of Bolivia beyond the city limits. Here are some of the top day trips you can take from La Paz:

**Tiwanaku Archaeological Site:** Located approximately 72 kilometers (45 miles) west of La Paz, the Tiwanaku archaeological site is one of Bolivia's most significant pre-Columbian sites and a UNESCO World Heritage Site. This ancient city was once the center of the Tiwanaku civilization, which thrived between 300 and 1000 AD. The site is famous for its impressive stone structures and intricate carvings, which showcase the advanced engineering and architectural skills of its inhabitants.

Visitors to Tiwanaku can explore the remains of the Puma Punku, known for its massive stone blocks that fit together with remarkable precision. The Akapana Pyramid, another key feature of the site, offers a glimpse into the ceremonial practices of the Tiwanaku people. Guided tours are available and often provide insightful information about the site's history and significance.

The nearby Tiwanaku Museum further enriches the experience by displaying artifacts excavated from the site, including pottery, textiles, and stone tools. A visit to Tiwanaku not only allows you to witness the impressive ruins but also provides an opportunity to learn about one of the ancient civilizations that shaped the region.

**Moon Valley:** Just a short drive from La Paz, Moon Valley (Valle de la Luna) offers a surreal landscape that feels like stepping onto another planet. This unique geological formation, located about 10 kilometers (6 miles) from the city, is characterized by its striking erosion patterns, which have created a series of valleys and spires resembling a lunar landscape. The formations are primarily made of clay, sand, and silt, resulting in a palette of earthy tones that change with the light throughout the day.

Visitors can explore the area through a network of walking trails that provide stunning viewpoints over the valley. The site is particularly beautiful during sunset when the colors of the rocks become more vibrant. There is also a small visitor center with information about the geological processes that formed the valley. Moon Valley is ideal for a quick escape from the hustle and bustle of La Paz, offering a peaceful and otherworldly experience.

**Lake Titicaca:** Lake Titicaca, the highest navigable lake in the world, is located about 70 kilometers (43 miles) from La Paz and is a must-see destination for any traveler in the region. Known for its deep blue waters and stunning mountain backdrop, the lake is a spiritual and cultural hub for the indigenous Aymara and Quechua people. A day trip to Lake Titicaca typically includes a visit to Isla del Sol (Island of the Sun) or Isla de la Luna (Island of the Moon), both of which hold significant cultural importance and breathtaking scenery.

On Isla del Sol, you can explore ancient Incan ruins, hike along well-marked trails, and enjoy panoramic views of the lake and surrounding mountains. The island is dotted with small villages where you can experience local life, taste traditional food, and interact with the welcoming inhabitants. The journey to the island often involves a scenic boat ride, adding to the overall experience.

For a more relaxed visit, you can also explore the lakeside town of Copacabana, known for its beautiful beaches and the famous Basilica of Our Lady of Copacabana, a pilgrimage site for many Bolivians. Here, you can enjoy fresh fish dishes from the lake and soak in the tranquil atmosphere.

**Chacaltaya and Huayna Potosí:** For adventure seekers, a day trip to the Chacaltaya Glacier and Huayna Potosí offers breathtaking views and exhilarating hiking opportunities. Chacaltaya, located about 30 kilometers (19 miles) from La Paz, is accessible by vehicle, making it a great option for those looking to enjoy high-altitude scenery without extensive trekking.

Once at Chacaltaya, visitors can take in panoramic views of the surrounding mountains, including Huayna Potosí, which towers at 6,088 meters (19,974 feet). For more adventurous travelers, Huayna Potosí offers climbing expeditions that can be arranged locally. Although the climb is challenging, experienced guides provide assistance and support, making it achievable for those in good physical condition.

For those who prefer a more leisurely experience, hiking around Chacaltaya allows you to explore the unique flora and fauna of the Altiplano while taking in the stunning vistas of the Andes.

El Choro Trek: For those who enjoy hiking and outdoor activities, the El Choro Trek is a fantastic option that begins just a short drive from La Paz. This historic trek takes you through diverse landscapes, ranging from high Andean mountains to lush cloud forests, over the course of three days. However, many travelers choose to do a condensed version, completing a section of the trek in a day.

The trek follows an ancient Incan route, providing not only stunning views but also a glimpse into the region's history and culture. Along the way, trekkers will encounter small indigenous villages where they can learn about local customs and traditions. The combination of natural beauty and cultural immersion makes the El Choro Trek a memorable adventure.

While it is possible to hike this route independently, many travelers opt for guided tours that include transportation and meals, ensuring a safe and enjoyable experience.

La Paz is a gateway to some of Bolivia's most remarkable sights and experiences, making it an ideal base for day trips that cater to a variety of interests. Whether you're exploring ancient ruins, experiencing breathtaking landscapes, or engaging in adventurous outdoor activities, each day trip offers a unique perspective on the diverse beauty and rich culture of Bolivia. With so much to see and do, your time in La Paz will be filled with unforgettable adventures that showcase the essence of this captivating country.

EL CHORO TREK

# CHAPTER FOUR
# SALAR DE UYUNI

Salar de Uyuni, the world's largest salt flat, is a mesmerizing expanse that stretches over 10,000 square kilometers (3,900 square miles) in southwest Bolivia. This natural wonder is located at an elevation of 3,656 meters (11,995 feet) and is known for its striking white crust of salt that

creates an otherworldly landscape. Formed from the remnants of ancient lakes, the salt flat is not only a breathtaking sight but also a vital resource for lithium extraction. Travelers flock to Uyuni for its surreal beauty, especially during the rainy season (November to March), when a thin layer of water transforms the flat into a vast mirror, reflecting the sky in a spectacular display of blues and whites.

Exploring Salar de Uyuni is an adventure like no other, offering visitors a chance to witness unique geological formations, such as the iconic Isla Incahuasi, a rocky outcrop covered in giant cacti that rises dramatically from the salt plain. In addition to its stunning visuals, the area is rich in biodiversity, home to various species of flamingos that inhabit the surrounding lagoons. Tours to Uyuni often include visits to the nearby train graveyard, where rusting locomotives tell stories of Bolivia's railway history. Whether you're standing in the middle of the vast salt flat, taking in the vastness of the landscape, or capturing the perfect photo of the reflective surface, a visit to Salar de Uyuni promises to be an unforgettable highlight of any Bolivian adventure.

# EXPLORING THE SALT FLATS

Salar de Uyuni, the world's largest salt flat, is one of Bolivia's most iconic and breathtaking destinations. Exploring this vast, alien-like landscape offers travelers a chance to experience nature in its purest form, with surreal, seemingly infinite white expanses that stretch to the horizon. Whether you're visiting during the dry season or the rainy season, each time of year offers a distinct and awe-inspiring experience.

**Dry Season:** During the dry season (May to October), Salar de Uyuni transforms into a never-ending plain of solid salt. The ground beneath your feet is cracked and patterned in unique hexagonal shapes formed by the natural drying process. The horizon becomes difficult to distinguish, and the flat, white surface seems to merge with the sky in all directions, creating an almost dizzying effect. The salt crust is thick enough to drive on, and most tours traverse this expansive plain in sturdy 4x4 vehicles, allowing travelers to explore deeper into the flat.

Exploring the salt flats during this time provides opportunities for creative photography. Due to the lack of visual markers and the flat surface, playing with perspectives is a popular activity here. Tourists often use small props to create optical illusion photos that make objects or people appear much larger or smaller than they really are. This playful interaction with the landscape adds a unique and fun aspect to the adventure.

Aside from the flat itself, one of the highlights of the dry season is visiting Isla Incahuasi, also known as the "Cactus Island." Located in the middle of the salt flat, this hilly island is covered in massive cacti that can grow up to 12 meters (40 feet) tall. The island offers a stark contrast to the flat, barren surroundings and provides a panoramic view of the vast salt flats from its summit. Hiking up Incahuasi is a must-do, as it reveals the sheer scale and beauty of the Salar.

**Rainy Season:** Between November and March, the rainy season transforms Salar de Uyuni into a massive natural mirror. A thin layer of water covers the salt flat, creating a reflective surface that mirrors the sky above, blending seamlessly into the horizon. This creates the illusion of walking on the sky and is an experience unlike any other on Earth. The reflections are particularly stunning at sunrise and sunset when the sky is painted with hues of orange, pink, and purple, making the salt flats appear even more ethereal.

During the rainy season, 4x4 tours still operate, but the routes may change depending on the water levels. Many travelers come specifically for this phenomenon, as the photographs and memories of standing on the "mirror of the sky" are unforgettable. This natural wonder is a photographer's dream, and the contrast between the dark storm clouds or the bright blue sky reflected on the white surface creates a stunning visual experience.

**The Train Graveyard and Salt Hotels:** Exploring the salt flats often begins with a visit to the nearby train graveyard, located just outside the town of Uyuni. This site is home to rusted and abandoned steam locomotives from the early 20th century, remnants of Bolivia's once-thriving mining industry. These old trains were used to transport minerals to the Pacific coast, but when the industry declined, they were left to decay in the harsh salt desert environment. Today, the train graveyard offers a glimpse into Bolivia's industrial past and serves as a popular spot for atmospheric, historical photos.

Another unique aspect of visiting Salar de Uyuni is staying in one of the salt hotels scattered around the perimeter of the flat. These structures are built entirely from blocks of salt, including the walls, floors, and even the furniture. The Palacio de Sal, for example, is a famous hotel that offers luxury accommodations in an entirely salt-made building, giving guests a truly one-of-a-kind experience. Staying in a salt hotel provides insight into the resourcefulness of the local community and the significance of salt to the region.

**Wildlife and Surrounding Landscapes:** While Salar de Uyuni is known for its stark beauty, the area surrounding the salt flats is also rich in biodiversity and varied landscapes. During the rainy season, the salt flats become a vital breeding ground for thousands of flamingos, particularly the Andean, Chilean, and James's flamingo species. These vibrant birds create a striking contrast against the white salt and blue sky, making them a major draw for wildlife enthusiasts and photographers.

On the edges of the flats, you'll find several picturesque lagunas (lagoons), including the famous Laguna Colorada and Laguna Verde. These multi-colored lakes, filled with rich mineral content, are framed by dramatic volcanic backdrops. The colors of these lagoons change depending on the time of day and the concentration of minerals, offering a vibrant spectacle in contrast to the white salt flats. Laguna Colorada, in particular, is known for its red hue, which is caused by algae in the water, and its large population of flamingos that gather along its shores.

**The Salt Extraction Process:** While exploring Salar de Uyuni, visitors also get the chance to learn about the traditional methods of salt extraction that have been practiced by the local people for centuries. The salt is collected in small piles, which are left to dry in the sun before being processed and sold. Salt harvesting is still an important livelihood for many communities around the flats, and tours often stop at one of the salt mining areas to explain the process.

In recent years, the salt flat has gained further importance due to its massive deposits of lithium, a mineral crucial for the production of batteries for electronics and electric vehicles. Bolivia holds the world's largest lithium reserves, and while the salt flat is still predominantly a tourist attraction, its future role in the global lithium industry is set to grow significantly.

**Multi-Day Tours and Stargazing:** While many visitors opt for a one-day tour of Salar de Uyuni, multi-day tours are also popular and offer a more immersive experience. These longer tours typically include visits to the nearby Eduardo Avaroa National Park, home to the famous geysers of Sol de Mañana and the unique stone tree formation, as well as several high-altitude lakes. Travelers on these extended tours can experience the diverse beauty of Bolivia's Altiplano region, which includes surreal desert landscapes, volcanic hot springs, and the famous Dali Desert with its otherworldly rock formations.

Another highlight of an overnight tour is stargazing on the salt flats. Due to the lack of light pollution and the high altitude, the sky over Uyuni is incredibly clear, offering some of the best stargazing conditions in the world. On a clear night, you can see the Milky Way stretching across the sky, as well as countless stars and constellations, creating a magical atmosphere that adds to the otherworldly experience of the salt flats.

Exploring Salar de Uyuni is a once-in-a-lifetime experience that offers travelers a chance to witness one of the most unique landscapes on Earth. Whether you visit during the dry season and marvel at the endless white expanse or come during the rainy season to walk on the world's largest natural mirror, the salt flats will leave you in awe. From visiting Isla Incahuasi and the train graveyard to experiencing the wildlife, salt hotels, and surrounding lagoons, there is so much to explore in this unforgettable part of Bolivia.

# VISITING INCAHUASI ISLAND

Incahuasi Island, also known as Isla Incahuasi, is one of the most unique and striking landmarks within Bolivia's Salar de Uyuni. This small, rocky island emerges unexpectedly from the vast, white expanse of the salt flats, creating an astonishing contrast with its surrounding landscape. Often referred to as "Cactus Island" because of the towering cacti that cover its terrain, Incahuasi offers visitors not only a stunning natural spectacle but also a fascinating insight into the region's geology, flora, and ancient history.

**A Geological Marvel in a Sea of Salt:** Incahuasi Island is a remnant of a time long past when the salt flats were once a vast prehistoric lake known as Lake Minchin. As the water evaporated, it left behind this elevated coral island, which today stands in the middle of the world's largest salt flat. The island's ancient coral rock formations give evidence of its underwater past, and as you walk along its trails, you can observe fossilized remnants embedded in the terrain. The combination of coral rock and massive cacti growing out of this barren environment creates an otherworldly scene, making it one of the most visually striking stops on any tour of Salar de Uyuni.

The island rises about 100 meters (330 feet) above the salt flat, and from the top, you are treated to panoramic views of the endless white expanse below. The hike to the summit is short but rewarding, offering a 360-degree perspective that truly captures the vastness of Salar de Uyuni. As you look out, the salt flat stretches to the horizon in every direction, creating the surreal illusion of an infinite white desert.

2. **Towering Cacti:** Perhaps the most remarkable feature of Incahuasi Island is the thousands of giant Trichocereus cacti that dot the landscape. These massive cacti can grow up to 12 meters (40 feet) in height and are estimated to be over 1,000 years old. The resilience of these plants, thriving in such an extreme and arid environment, is a testament to nature's adaptability. The towering cacti provide a sharp contrast to the stark whiteness of the surrounding salt flats, their green spines jutting upward against the clear blue sky.

As you explore the island, you'll notice that these cacti dominate every part of the rocky landscape, with some growing in seemingly impossible places. They are the island's only significant plant life, adding to the feeling of isolation and remoteness that Incahuasi exudes. Walking among these ancient giants, you can't help but marvel at the way they have stood sentinel over the island for centuries, with some of the oldest specimens reaching ages well over a millennium.

The cacti also play an important ecological role, providing shelter and sustenance for the local wildlife, including birds and insects. During certain times of the year, the cacti bloom with bright white flowers, further enhancing the island's rugged beauty and adding a touch of color to the otherwise monochromatic landscape.

**Ancient Inca Legacy and Local Legends:** Incahuasi Island holds cultural and historical significance as well. Its name, Incahuasi, translates to "House of the Inca" in Quechua, a reference to the island's connection to ancient Andean civilizations. According to local legend, the island was a sacred place for the Inca, and remnants of their presence can still be felt today. Though no formal ruins exist on the island, it is believed that the island served as a spiritual refuge for ancient peoples who inhabited the area long before the salt flats became the desolate landscape we see today.

The indigenous Aymara people, who have lived in the region for centuries, also consider the island to be a sacred site. Incahuasi, along with other islands in the Salar de Uyuni, is part of the broader Andean cosmovision that views natural landscapes as living entities. The salt flats themselves, for example, are seen as an important spiritual and cultural marker, and Incahuasi Island is imbued with this mystical significance.

In modern times, the island has become a popular stop for tourists exploring Salar de Uyuni, and local guides often share stories and legends about the island's role in the spiritual beliefs of the indigenous peoples. The history, combined with the dramatic scenery, creates a sense of awe and reverence as you explore its paths.

**Exploring the Island:** Visitors to Incahuasi Island have the opportunity to explore the island's well-marked hiking trails, which wind through its rocky landscape and dense cactus groves. The main trail leads to the island's summit, offering spectacular views of the surrounding salt flats. The hike is not particularly strenuous, but the island's elevation—standing at around 3,650 meters (12,000 feet) above sea level—can make even moderate physical exertion feel more challenging due to the thinner air. However, the reward at the top is well worth the effort.

From the island's highest point, the panorama of Salar de Uyuni is breathtaking. The seemingly endless white landscape, stretching in every direction, is best appreciated from this vantage point, where the salt flats' flatness and vastness are fully revealed. On clear days, the horizon blends into the sky, creating an optical illusion where the ground and the heavens appear to merge. The isolation and silence at the summit add to the surreal experience, making it a perfect spot for reflection and photography.

Visitors often spend time here soaking in the views, taking photos, and listening to local guides share the island's geological and cultural history. The uniqueness of the landscape makes Incahuasi Island a popular destination for travelers seeking to understand the broader natural and human history of the salt flats.

**Photography Opportunities:** Incahuasi Island is a dream location for photographers, whether amateur or professional. The contrasting elements of the island's landscape—white salt flats, towering cacti, rocky formations, and deep blue skies—provide a striking backdrop for stunning photographs. Many visitors take advantage of the wide, flat expanse of the surrounding salt flats to create optical illusion photos with the island's dramatic features in the background.

During the rainy season, when Salar de Uyuni becomes a mirror-like surface, the reflections add another layer of complexity and beauty to the photographs taken from the island. The clear reflections of the island, cacti, and sky in the shallow water create an almost magical scene, enhancing the otherworldly feeling of the place.

Whether you're a casual photographer capturing the beauty of nature or a professional seeking to frame the perfect shot, Incahuasi Island provides a wealth of opportunities to create memorable images.

**The Island's Ecosystem and Conservation Efforts:** Despite its remote and seemingly desolate environment, Incahuasi Island supports a fragile ecosystem. In addition to the towering cacti, the island is home to various species of birds, insects, and small mammals. The cacti, as the dominant plant life, play a crucial role in sustaining this ecosystem, providing food and shelter for the island's inhabitants.

Due to the increasing number of tourists visiting Salar de Uyuni and Incahuasi Island, there are ongoing conservation efforts to protect the island's delicate environment. Visitors are encouraged to stay on designated paths, avoid disturbing the wildlife, and respect the natural surroundings. Guides and locals work together to ensure that tourism is conducted in a sustainable manner, preserving this unique landscape for future generations to enjoy.

Visiting Incahuasi Island is an unforgettable part of any trip to Salar de Uyuni. Its dramatic landscape, towering cacti, and panoramic views of the salt flats make it one of the most remarkable and surreal destinations in Bolivia. Whether you're drawn to its geological wonders, its cultural history, or the stunning vistas it offers, Incahuasi Island is a must-see for anyone exploring the Uyuni region. It stands as a reminder of the power and beauty of nature, offering visitors a unique experience that combines adventure, reflection, and awe.

# SALT HOTELS AND UNIQUE ACCOMMODATIONS

One of the most unique aspects of staying near the Salar de Uyuni is the availability of salt hotels—accommodations built almost entirely from blocks of salt harvested from the nearby flats. These salt hotels provide an experience unlike any other, allowing guests to stay in structures that blend into the surreal landscape of the world's largest salt flat. In addition to these salt hotels, there are a number of eco-friendly lodges and boutique accommodations that offer a distinct Bolivian charm, catering to travelers seeking both comfort and adventure. Here's an in-depth look at the unique accommodations available in Salar de Uyuni.

**Salt Hotels:** One of the most fascinating types of lodging in Salar de Uyuni is the salt hotel. These extraordinary structures are built using salt bricks, giving them a white, crystalline appearance that harmonizes perfectly with the surrounding salt flats. From the walls to the furniture—beds, chairs, and tables—almost everything is crafted from salt. These hotels offer a one-of-a-kind experience where guests can fully immerse themselves in the magic of Salar de Uyuni.

The most famous of these is the Palacio de Sal, often considered the world's first hotel built entirely from salt. Located near the edge of the salt flats, this luxurious property provides a balance of comfort and surreal design, creating a stay that feels more like a dream than reality. Each room is crafted from salt blocks and features minimalist yet elegant decor, ensuring that guests have a comfortable stay while admiring the beauty of their surroundings. The hotel's common areas, including a dining room, bar, and lounge, are also built from salt, giving the entire property a cohesive and otherworldly aesthetic. The Palacio de Sal offers luxury amenities like a spa, sauna, and even a saltwater pool, making it an ideal choice for travelers looking to unwind after exploring the flats.

Another notable salt hotel is Luna Salada Hotel, a more boutique option known for its cozy atmosphere and stunning views of the salt flats. Luna Salada is perched on a small hill, offering panoramic vistas of the vast white landscape. Like Palacio de Sal, the hotel is constructed almost entirely from salt blocks, and its design reflects the natural beauty of the region. The rooms are comfortable and stylish, featuring Andean textiles and wooden accents that create a warm, inviting environment despite the harsh conditions outside. Luna Salada also has an on-site restaurant that serves local Bolivian cuisine, with ingredients sourced from nearby farms and markets. This hotel is perfect for those who want to enjoy a tranquil and intimate stay with close access to the salt flats.

Staying in a salt hotel offers more than just a place to sleep—it's a cultural and sensory experience. Walking through hallways made of salt, sleeping in a salt bed, and even eating in a salt-walled dining room immerses you in the uniqueness of Salar de Uyuni. The hotels maintain the integrity of their surroundings by embracing the natural resources of the area in their construction and design. Despite being made from salt, these hotels manage to offer modern amenities like heating, electricity, and Wi-Fi, ensuring that guests can enjoy both comfort and novelty.

**Eco-Friendly Lodges:** For travelers looking for accommodations that prioritize sustainability and environmental stewardship, there are several eco-friendly lodges around Salar de Uyuni that offer unique and responsible options. These lodges are designed to minimize their impact on the fragile ecosystem of the salt flats, incorporating sustainable building practices, renewable energy, and responsible waste management into their operations.

Kachi Lodge stands out as one of the most eco-friendly and luxurious options near Salar de Uyuni. Located directly on the salt flats, Kachi Lodge offers futuristic dome-shaped accommodations that blend seamlessly with the landscape. The lodge features a series of geodesic domes raised on wooden platforms, providing stunning views of the salt flats while minimizing environmental impact. Each dome is equipped with modern comforts like plush bedding, heating, and private bathrooms, allowing guests to enjoy a comfortable stay in one of the world's most remote locations. Kachi Lodge is entirely solar-powered and uses sustainable materials in its construction, making it one of the most environmentally responsible lodging options in the region. In addition to its eco-friendly focus, the lodge also offers gourmet meals prepared by top Bolivian chefs, often using locally sourced ingredients.

Another eco-conscious option is the Ecolodge Los Flamencos, which is located near the Reserva Nacional de Fauna Andina Eduardo Avaroa, a protected area known for its wildlife, including flamingos. The lodge is built using local materials and follows strict sustainability guidelines to minimize its environmental footprint. Los Flamencos is situated near the breathtaking Laguna Colorada, a red-tinted lake famous for its flamingo population, offering guests the chance to explore Bolivia's natural beauty while staying in eco-friendly accommodations. The lodge provides comfortable rooms with solar-powered electricity, water conservation systems, and locally crafted furnishings, ensuring that guests can experience nature without compromising on comfort.

These eco-lodges emphasize the importance of responsible tourism in fragile environments like Salar de Uyuni, offering travelers the chance to explore Bolivia's incredible landscapes while supporting sustainability efforts. By staying in one of these lodges, you can enjoy a unique and luxurious experience while knowing that your visit is helping to preserve the area's natural beauty for future generations.

**Unique Boutique Hotels:** Beyond salt hotels and eco-lodges, Salar de Uyuni and its surrounding areas are home to a number of boutique hotels that offer a unique blend of local culture, luxury, and personalized service. These smaller, independent hotels often reflect the spirit of the region through their design, hospitality, and cuisine, providing guests with a more intimate and authentic experience.

Hotel de Sal Cristal Samaña is one such example, offering a boutique experience that combines traditional Andean architecture with modern comforts. Located just outside the town of Colchani, the gateway to Salar de Uyuni, the hotel features rooms and suites constructed from salt blocks, with designs that incorporate local textiles, artisan crafts, and warm earthy tones. The hotel's emphasis on local culture is reflected in its attentive service and the traditional Bolivian dishes served at its restaurant, which uses fresh ingredients sourced from the region. With its proximity to the salt flats and local attractions, Cristal Samaña is an excellent choice for travelers who want to combine convenience with cultural immersion.

Another standout option is the Hotel Jardines de Uyuni, a charming boutique hotel located in the town of Uyuni itself. This hotel offers a more urban setting, making it a convenient base for exploring the salt flats and surrounding areas. The design of Jardines de Uyuni blends rustic charm with modern amenities, featuring cozy rooms decorated with local art and textiles. The hotel's restaurant is renowned for its traditional Bolivian dishes, and the courtyard offers a peaceful retreat after a day of exploration. Despite its central location, Jardines de Uyuni provides a calm, intimate atmosphere, making it ideal for travelers who want a more personalized and culturally rich stay.

These unique boutique hotels provide travelers with a more personalized experience than larger, chain hotels. Their emphasis on local culture, art, and cuisine makes them an excellent choice for those looking to connect with the spirit of the Uyuni region while enjoying the comforts of modern hospitality.

Whether you choose to stay in a salt hotel, an eco-friendly lodge, or a boutique hotel, the accommodations around Salar de Uyuni offer some of the most unique lodging experiences in the world. Each option provides a distinct way to engage with the surreal landscape, from sleeping in rooms made of salt to enjoying sustainable luxury in the heart of nature. These hotels and lodges not only provide a comfortable place to rest but also enhance your overall experience in one of Bolivia's most iconic destinations, ensuring that your visit to Salar de Uyuni is as unforgettable as the salt flats themselves.

COCHABAMBA

# CHAPTER FIVE
# POTOSÍ AND SUCRE

Nestled in the heart of the Andes, Potosí and Sucre are two captivating cities that showcase Bolivia's rich history and vibrant culture. Potosí, once one of the wealthiest cities in the world due to its silver mines, offers a glimpse into the colonial past with its stunning architecture and historic sites. Visitors can explore the infamous Cerro Rico mountain, where countless miners worked in grueling conditions, and delve into the city's history at the Casa de la Moneda, the former mint that produced coins for the Spanish Empire. The city's unique blend of indigenous and colonial influences creates a fascinating atmosphere that invites exploration and reflection on its tumultuous past.

Just a short journey away, Sucre serves as Bolivia's constitutional capital and is known for its beautifully preserved colonial architecture and serene ambiance. This charming city is often referred to as the "White City" due to its stunning white-washed buildings and picturesque plazas. Sucre is home to important cultural institutions, including the Universidad de San Francisco Xavier, one of the oldest universities in the Americas, and the vibrant Mercado Central, where visitors can savor local delicacies and shop for handcrafted souvenirs. Together, Potosí and Sucre provide a rich tapestry of history, culture, and tradition, making them must-visit destinations for anyone exploring Bolivia.

# HISTORY OF POTOSÍ

The history of Potosí is intricately tied to the discovery of silver in the Cerro Rico mountain, which looms majestically over the city. Founded in 1545, Potosí quickly rose to prominence as one of the wealthiest cities in the world due to its vast silver deposits, attracting adventurers, miners, and fortune seekers from all over the Spanish Empire. The city became a focal point of colonial wealth, providing a substantial portion of Spain's silver supply and contributing significantly to the global economy of the 16th and 17th centuries. At its height, Potosí was one of the largest cities in the world, boasting a population that rivaled that of London or Paris at the time, with estimates suggesting it housed over 200,000 inhabitants.

The discovery of silver transformed Potosí into a bustling center of commerce and culture. Wealth flowed into the city, leading to the construction of magnificent colonial buildings, churches, and palaces, many of which still stand today. The city became a melting pot of cultures, where Spanish colonists, indigenous peoples, and enslaved Africans mingled. However, the prosperity of Potosí came at a significant cost. The indigenous population was subjected to harsh labor conditions in the mines, where many worked under the "mita" system—a forced labor draft that exploited native workers. The notorious Cerro Rico mines were notorious for their perilous conditions, with countless miners losing their lives due to accidents, exhaustion, or mercury poisoning.

As the 17th century progressed, the silver production began to decline, leading to economic instability in Potosí. By the 18th century, the city faced significant challenges, including political unrest, resource depletion, and changing trade routes. However, Potosí's rich history continued to shape its identity. In 1825, Potosí played a crucial role in Bolivia's independence from Spanish rule, serving as a stronghold for revolutionary forces. Despite its decline, the city's historical significance and cultural heritage remained intact, earning it a place as a UNESCO World Heritage site in 1987.

Today, Potosí stands as a testament to Bolivia's colonial past and the resilience of its people. Visitors can explore its cobblestone streets, admire the stunning architecture, and delve into the history of its silver mines. The city also reflects the enduring legacy of its indigenous population and the impact of colonialism, with vibrant traditions and customs that continue to thrive. Museums, such as the Casa de la Moneda and the Museo de Potosí, offer insights into the city's storied past, while the local markets and festivals showcase the rich cultural tapestry that defines Potosí today. The history of Potosí serves as a reminder of both the immense wealth generated from its resources and the human cost of such prosperity, making it a fascinating destination for those seeking to understand Bolivia's complex heritage.

# ATTRACTIONS IN SUCRE

Sucre, the constitutional capital of Bolivia, is renowned for its well-preserved colonial architecture, rich cultural heritage, and vibrant atmosphere. As a UNESCO World Heritage site, the city boasts a plethora of attractions that reflect its historical significance and artistic vibrancy. Visitors to Sucre will find an array of sites that highlight its unique character and cultural offerings.

1. **Plaza 25 de Mayo:** At the heart of Sucre lies Plaza 25 de Mayo, the city's main square and a hub of social and cultural life. Surrounded by stunning colonial buildings, including the Palacio de la Libertad, which was once the site of significant historical events during Bolivia's fight for independence, the plaza is an ideal place to soak in the local atmosphere. The square is adorned with beautifully landscaped gardens, fountains, and benches, making it a popular gathering spot for both locals and visitors. The vibrant market stalls and street performers that often populate the area add to the lively ambiance, making it a perfect starting point for exploring the city.

2. **The Cathedral of Sucre:** Dominating the skyline of Plaza 25 de Mayo is the Cathedral of Sucre, known for its striking white facade and stunning baroque architecture. Completed in 1712, the cathedral is a masterpiece of colonial design and reflects the influence of Spanish architecture in Bolivia. Inside, visitors can admire the ornate altars, beautiful frescoes, and intricate woodwork that tell the story of the city's religious heritage. The cathedral also houses a museum where guests can explore religious artifacts, paintings, and historical documents that provide insights into Sucre's spiritual history.

3. **Casa de la Libertad:** The Casa de la Libertad, or House of Liberty, is one of Sucre's most significant historical landmarks. This colonial building served as the meeting place for revolutionary leaders during Bolivia's struggle for independence from Spanish rule in the early 19th century. Today, it operates as a museum dedicated to Bolivia's fight for freedom and its path to becoming a sovereign nation. Visitors can explore the various rooms filled with historical artifacts, documents, and paintings that illustrate the story of Bolivia's independence. The highlight of the visit is the room where the Declaration of Independence was signed on August 6, 1825, making it a must-visit for history enthusiasts.

4. **Tarabuco Market:** A short drive from Sucre, the Tarabuco Market offers a glimpse into the traditional indigenous culture of Bolivia. Held every Sunday, this vibrant market is famous for its colorful textiles, handmade crafts, and local produce. Visitors can wander through the stalls, engage with local artisans, and sample traditional foods while enjoying the lively atmosphere. The market is also a fantastic opportunity to learn about the indigenous Yampara culture, as many of the vendors wear traditional clothing and are eager to share their stories and traditions with visitors.

5. **Recoleta Convent and Museum:** Perched on a hill overlooking Sucre, the Recoleta Convent offers breathtaking views of the city and the surrounding landscape. Founded in the 17th century, this historic convent is home to a museum that showcases a remarkable collection of colonial art, including religious paintings, sculptures, and artifacts. The tranquil gardens and beautiful architecture make it a peaceful retreat from the bustling city. Visitors

can explore the cloisters and learn about the history of the convent, making it a perfect spot for reflection and appreciation of Sucre's artistic heritage.

6. **University of San Francisco Xavier:** As one of the oldest universities in the Americas, the Universidad de San Francisco Xavier is a significant educational institution in Bolivia. Established in 1624, the university has played a crucial role in the cultural and intellectual development of the country. Visitors can explore the beautiful campus, which features impressive colonial architecture and a rich history. The university also hosts several cultural events and exhibitions throughout the year, allowing visitors to engage with local students and artists.

7. **Cretaceous Park (Parque Cretácico):** For those interested in paleontology, Cretaceous Park is a fascinating attraction located just outside Sucre. This unique park features one of the largest collections of dinosaur footprints in the world, preserved in a natural setting. Visitors can take guided tours to learn about the history of the dinosaurs that roamed the region millions of years ago, as well as the significance of the footprints in understanding the prehistoric era. The park also offers educational displays and activities that engage both children and adults in the wonders of paleontology.

Sucre's charm lies in its rich blend of history, culture, and natural beauty. Whether wandering through its picturesque streets, exploring its museums, or engaging with local traditions, visitors are sure to be captivated by the city's vibrant spirit and historical significance. The attractions in Sucre provide an enriching experience that highlights the heart and soul of Bolivia.

# CULTURAL EVENTS AND FESTIVALS

Sucre, the constitutional capital of Bolivia, is not only a city steeped in history but also a vibrant cultural hub that celebrates its rich heritage through a variety of events and festivals throughout the year. These celebrations offer visitors an authentic glimpse into the customs, traditions, and artistic expressions of the local population. The cultural events in Sucre are marked by colorful parades, traditional music, dance performances, and culinary delights, making them a highlight for anyone looking to experience the city's unique spirit.

1. **Carnaval de Sucre:** One of the most celebrated festivals in Sucre is the Carnaval de Sucre, which takes place in the days leading up to Ash Wednesday. This lively event features a series of parades, street parties, and cultural performances that transform the city into a vibrant spectacle of color and sound. Local residents don traditional costumes, often adorned with intricate embroidery and vivid colors, as they participate in spirited dance and music. The festival is characterized by playful water fights, where revelers throw water balloons and spray each other with water, creating a joyful and festive atmosphere. Traditional foods and beverages are also an integral part of the celebration, with stalls offering local delicacies such as salteñas (savory pastries) and chicha (a fermented corn drink). Carnaval de Sucre is a time for community bonding, showcasing the city's rich cultural tapestry and inviting visitors to join in the revelry.

2. **Fiesta de la Virgen de Guadalupe:** The Fiesta de la Virgen de Guadalupe, held in early September, is a significant religious celebration dedicated to the

patron saint of Sucre, Our Lady of Guadalupe. This event attracts thousands of devotees and visitors who come to honor the Virgin with colorful processions, traditional music, and vibrant dances. The festivities begin with a solemn mass at the Cathedral of Sucre, followed by a lively procession through the streets, where participants carry elaborate altars adorned with flowers and religious icons. Traditional folkloric groups perform dances that reflect the blend of indigenous and Spanish influences, celebrating the cultural heritage of the region. Street vendors line the route, offering a variety of local foods and crafts, creating a festive atmosphere that captivates both locals and tourists alike.

3. **Semana Santa (Holy Week):** Semana Santa, or Holy Week, is one of the most important religious observances in Bolivia, and Sucre celebrates it with great devotion and grandeur. From Palm Sunday to Easter Sunday, the city hosts a series of processions, masses, and rituals that commemorate the passion and resurrection of Jesus Christ. The streets come alive with the sights and sounds of solemn processions, where participants dressed in traditional robes carry statues of saints and religious icons. The dramatic re-enactments of biblical events, combined with the haunting melodies of choirs and the scent of incense, create an atmosphere of reflection and reverence. The Semana Santa celebrations culminate in the joyous Easter Sunday mass, marking the resurrection with an uplifting spirit that resonates throughout the city.

4. **Feria de Sucre:** The Feria de Sucre, typically held in November, is an annual fair that showcases the city's agricultural and artisanal products. This vibrant event features stalls displaying handmade crafts, textiles, and local produce, allowing artisans and farmers to promote their goods to a broader audience. Visitors can explore a wide array of traditional foods, from street snacks to gourmet offerings, providing a delicious way to experience the local cuisine. The fair also includes live music, dance performances, and cultural presentations, making it a lively celebration of Sucre's cultural diversity and creativity. This event is an excellent opportunity for visitors to interact with local artisans and learn more about Bolivian traditions and craftsmanship.

5. **Festival Internacional de Teatro:** The Festival Internacional de Teatro (International Theater Festival) is an artistic event that draws theater

companies and performers from around the world to Sucre. Held biennially in October, the festival features a diverse lineup of performances, including drama, comedy, and experimental theater. It serves as a platform for both national and international artists to showcase their talents and engage with local audiences. Workshops, discussions, and Q&A sessions often accompany the performances, allowing participants to delve deeper into the world of theater and explore various artistic expressions. This festival is a celebration of creativity and cultural exchange, fostering a vibrant arts community in Sucre.

6. **La Fiesta de San Juan:** Celebrated on June 24th, La Fiesta de San Juan marks the winter solstice and is a blend of indigenous and Catholic traditions. The festival is characterized by bonfires, traditional music, and communal feasting. Locals gather to celebrate the changing season, with the bonfires symbolizing the sun's return and the promise of warmer days ahead. People often prepare special dishes, such as roasted meats and traditional breads, to share with family and friends. The atmosphere is filled with music and dance, as groups gather around the fire to celebrate and tell stories. Visitors are encouraged to join in the festivities, immersing themselves in the warmth and camaraderie of this traditional celebration.

Sucre's cultural events and festivals reflect the city's rich history and the resilience of its people. These celebrations are not just about the festivities; they embody the spirit of community, tradition, and cultural pride that defines Sucre. For visitors, participating in these events provides a unique opportunity to connect with the local culture and gain a deeper understanding of Bolivia's vibrant heritage. Whether you're dancing in the streets during Carnaval or savoring traditional foods at the Feria de Sucre, the cultural experiences in this enchanting city are sure to leave lasting memories.

# CHAPTER SIX
# AMAZON BASIN AND LAKE TITICACA

The Amazon Basin and Lake Titicaca are two of Bolivia's most captivating natural wonders, offering an incredible diversity of landscapes and experiences. The Amazon Basin, located in the northeastern region of Bolivia, is a sprawling rainforest teeming with  wildlife, vibrant ecosystems, and indigenous communities. It's a haven for nature enthusiasts and eco-tourists, offering opportunities for jungle treks, wildlife viewing, and river cruises along the many tributaries of the Amazon. The area is rich in biodiversity, with unique plant species, exotic animals, and indigenous cultures that have lived harmoniously with the forest for centuries. Exploring this region promises an unforgettable adventure into one of the most biodiverse places on Earth.

To the west, Lake Titicaca, the highest navigable lake in the world, offers a completely different, yet equally enchanting experience. This serene, crystal-clear body of water sits at an altitude of 3,800 meters above sea level, bordered by both Bolivia and Peru. The lake is home to ancient cultures, such as the Aymara and Quechua, and holds immense cultural and spiritual significance. Visitors can explore the floating islands of the Uros people, trek to the sacred Island of the Sun, and experience the stunning beauty of the surrounding Andean mountains. Together, the Amazon Basin and Lake Titicaca offer a unique combination of nature, culture, and adventure, making them must-visit destinations in Bolivia.

# MADIDI NATIONAL PARK

Madidi National Park is one of Bolivia's most pristine and biodiverse protected areas, located in the northwestern part of the country, within the Amazon Basin. Spanning an impressive 19,000 square kilometers, Madidi is a UNESCO Biosphere Reserve and is widely regarded as one of the most biologically rich parks in the world. The park is a critical part of the Amazonian ecosystem, acting as a sanctuary for countless species of flora and fauna, many of which are endemic or endangered. Its varied landscapes, which range from high-altitude Andean mountain peaks to lowland tropical rainforests, create diverse habitats that support an astounding range of wildlife.

1. **Biodiversity and Wildlife:** Madidi National Park is famous for its extraordinary biodiversity, which includes over 1,000 species of birds, more than 200 species of mammals, and an estimated 6,000 plant species. The park is home to some of the most iconic and elusive creatures of the Amazon, including

jaguars, pumas, giant river otters, and spectacled bears. Birdwatchers will be in paradise, with the park offering opportunities to spot rare species such as the Andean condor, harpy eagle, and scarlet macaw. The park's rivers are teeming with aquatic life, including caimans, freshwater dolphins, and various species of fish. For those with a keen interest in botany, the dense rainforests provide an incredible array of medicinal plants, orchids, and trees such as the towering Brazil nut tree, a critical part of the local economy and ecosystem.

2. **Ecological Zones:** One of the park's defining features is its wide variety of ecological zones, which range from the high-altitude cloud forests to the lowland tropical jungles. In the Andean foothills, you'll find cloud forests shrouded in mist, with rich vegetation and unique wildlife such as the golden poison dart frog and various species of monkeys. As you descend into the lower regions of the park, the ecosystem transforms into dense rainforest, with towering trees, fast-flowing rivers, and an explosion of life. The biodiversity across these different zones creates distinct ecological niches, allowing visitors to witness a range of ecosystems within one park. Madidi's watersheds, which feed into the Amazon River, are also crucial to the park's overall ecological health, providing a habitat for many species of aquatic life.

3. **Activities and Exploration:** The remote location and vast size of Madidi National Park make it a fantastic destination for eco-tourists and adventure seekers. Visitors to Madidi can embark on guided treks through the jungle, with local indigenous guides sharing their knowledge of the area's flora and fauna. These treks can range from short walks to multi-day hikes, depending on the level of adventure desired. For those interested in water-based activities, kayaking along the park's rivers offers a unique perspective of the rainforest and the opportunity to spot wildlife along the banks. Boat tours are a popular way to explore the park, with opportunities to spot river dolphins, birds, and other creatures that inhabit the waters. In addition, many eco-lodges are scattered throughout the park, offering immersive experiences that allow visitors to sleep under the stars and wake up to the sounds of the jungle.

4. **Indigenous Communities and Conservation Efforts:** Madidi is not only an ecological treasure but also a cultural one, as it is home to several indigenous communities that have lived in the region for centuries. These communities,

such as the Tacana, the Mosetén, and the Esse Ejja, have a deep spiritual connection to the land and are integral to the park's conservation efforts. Many indigenous people work as park rangers, guides, and conservationists, ensuring that traditional knowledge and practices are preserved while contributing to sustainable tourism. The park's management involves collaboration between the Bolivian government, local communities, and international organizations, ensuring that the ecological integrity of the park is maintained for future generations.

5. **Conservation and Challenges:** Despite its protected status, Madidi National Park faces ongoing challenges due to illegal logging, mining, and land encroachment. These activities threaten the park's delicate ecosystems and the livelihoods of its indigenous inhabitants. However, the park's remote location has helped preserve much of its natural beauty, and ongoing conservation efforts, including anti-poaching patrols and sustainable tourism practices, are making a positive impact. There is also a growing awareness of the importance of preserving the Amazon's ecosystems, as it plays a crucial role in global climate regulation and biodiversity conservation. Visiting Madidi National Park not only offers an opportunity to witness one of the world's most spectacular rainforests but also contributes to its ongoing preservation.

Madidi National Park is a true gem of Bolivia, offering unparalleled opportunities for wildlife observation, eco-tourism, and adventure. With its staggering biodiversity, stunning landscapes, and deep cultural significance, it stands as one of the last unspoiled frontiers of the Amazon rainforest. For those willing to embark on a journey to this remote part of the world, Madidi provides a once-in-a-lifetime opportunity to connect with nature in its purest form. Whether you're trekking through its jungle, spotting wildlife along its rivers, or learning about the ancient traditions of the indigenous communities, Madidi National Park is an unforgettable destination for any nature lover.

# VISITING ISLA DEL SOL AND ISLA DE LA LUNA

Bolivia's Lake Titicaca is not only known for its serene beauty but also for the fascinating islands that dot its expansive waters. Among the most iconic of these islands are Isla del Sol (Island of the Sun) and Isla de la Luna (Island of the Moon), two historically and culturally significant places that draw visitors from around the world. These islands, steeped in Inca mythology, offer stunning views, ancient ruins, and a glimpse into the spirituality of the Andean civilizations.

**Isla del Sol:** Isla del Sol is often considered the heart of Lake Titicaca and is one of Bolivia's most sacred and mystical places. According to Inca legend, it was on this island that the sun was born, making it a site of pilgrimage for the ancient Andean people. The island is located about 8 kilometers off the northern shore of Lake Titicaca, and its 14-square-kilometer area is home to a network of ancient Inca ruins, hiking trails, and breathtaking views.

1. **Inca Ruins and Archaeological Sites** Isla del Sol is a treasure trove of archaeological wonders. The island is home to several well-preserved Incan sites, most notably the Pilkokaina Palace—a ceremonial building that was once used by Inca royalty. As you wander through the island's paths, you'll also come across the Chincana ruins, a complex of stone structures that are believed to have been an important religious center for the Incas. The Inti Wata, or "Sun God" temple, is one of the most significant sites on the island, and it is often associated with the creation myth that the sun emerged from the island to light the world. Another fascinating site is the Sacred Rock (or Roca Sagrada), which is said to be the birthplace of the first Incan emperor, Manco Capac, according to Inca myth.

2. **Hiking and Scenic Views** Beyond its ruins, Isla del Sol is also renowned for its natural beauty. The island offers a variety of hiking opportunities, allowing visitors to explore its terraced hillsides, secluded beaches, and remote villages. The most famous trek is the Sun and Moon Trail, a scenic route that leads from the island's northern tip to its southern shores. The trail offers panoramic views of the vast Lake Titicaca, as well as the snow-capped peaks of the Andes in the distance. The island's pristine environment and tranquility make it an ideal place for reflection, spiritual rejuvenation, or simply taking in the beauty of one of the highest lakes in the world.

3. **Local Communities and Culture** The island is also home to small, traditional communities that have lived on Isla del Sol for centuries. The Aymara people, who are descendants of the ancient Andean civilizations, still maintain their traditional ways of life. Visitors to the island can interact with locals, learn about their farming practices, and explore their artisanal crafts. Many small guesthouses and family-run establishments offer a chance to experience the island's culture, providing visitors with a warm welcome and an authentic glimpse into daily life in this remote corner of Bolivia.

Isla de la Luna: Located just to the south of Isla del Sol, Isla de la Luna (Island of the Moon) is smaller and less visited but no less enchanting. Like Isla del Sol, Isla de la Luna is rich in Inca history and holds significant cultural and religious importance. It is said to have been the home of the Inca Virgins, women who were dedicated to the moon goddess, Mama Killa. While Isla de la Luna is not as developed for tourism as Isla del Sol, it remains a place of quiet spiritual significance, offering a more tranquil and serene environment for exploration.

1. **The Moon Temple** The most notable archaeological site on Isla de la Luna is the Temple of the Moon (or Iñak Uyu), which was used for ceremonial purposes by the Incas. This site, although more modest than the larger temples on Isla del Sol, still offers visitors an intriguing glimpse into the religious practices of the Inca civilization. The Moon Temple is believed to have been dedicated to Mama Killa, the goddess of the moon, and was likely used for lunar ceremonies and rituals. The island also houses the Inca Stairs,

a set of ancient stone steps that lead visitors up to the temple site, where they can enjoy sweeping views of Lake Titicaca and the surrounding Andes mountains.

2. **Natural Beauty and Hiking** Though Isla de la Luna is less developed, its natural beauty is no less captivating. The island is characterized by rocky shores, steep hills, and lush vegetation. Hiking on Isla de la Luna offers a quieter alternative to the more popular Isla del Sol, with the chance to explore its rugged terrain and enjoy uninterrupted views of the lake. Visitors can take a leisurely walk along the island's coast, soak in the peaceful atmosphere, and perhaps encounter the occasional local fisherman going about their daily routines. The island's isolation makes it an ideal place for those seeking a peaceful retreat, away from the crowds.

3. **Local Communities and Wildlife** Like Isla del Sol, Isla de la Luna is also home to a small community of Aymara-speaking people who live in harmony with their environment. Visitors can interact with the local residents and learn about their traditional way of life, including their agricultural practices and their deep spiritual connection to Lake Titicaca. The island is also home to a variety of bird species, particularly seabirds that nest along its cliffs. Birdwatchers will find Isla de la Luna to be an excellent spot to observe local wildlife, as the island's remote location and lack of tourism development have helped preserve its natural habitat.

Visiting Isla del Sol and Isla de la Luna is an unforgettable experience for those interested in history, culture, and nature. Whether you're exploring ancient Incan ruins, hiking through the scenic landscapes, or simply soaking in the mystical atmosphere of these sacred islands, they offer a unique glimpse into the spiritual and historical heart of the Andes. Both islands offer a peaceful respite from the bustling cities of Bolivia and provide an opportunity to connect with nature and ancient traditions. A visit to these two islands is a perfect way to experience the magic of Lake Titicaca, one of the most revered lakes in the world.

# ACTIVITIES ON THE LAKE

Lake Titicaca, perched high in the Andes, is the largest freshwater lake in South America by volume of water and surface area, and the highest navigable lake in the world. Its pristine blue waters, surrounded by stunning mountain landscapes, make it a perfect destination for a variety of water-based activities. Whether you seek adventure, relaxation, or cultural immersion, the lake offers a wealth of opportunities for every type of traveler. Here's a deeper dive into some of the most popular and exciting activities on Lake Titicaca:

**Boat Tours and Scenic Cruises:** One of the best ways to appreciate the sheer beauty of Lake Titicaca is by taking a boat tour. Several companies around the lake offer guided cruises, ranging from short excursions to multi-day trips, allowing visitors to experience the tranquil waters and breathtaking landscapes from a unique perspective. As you cruise along the lake's vast expanse, you'll be treated to panoramic views of the surrounding mountains, the distant snow-capped peaks of the Andes, and the scattered islands that dot the lake.

- **Private and Shared Tours:** For a more intimate experience, visitors can hire a private boat to explore the lake's many islands at their own pace, including popular destinations like Isla del Sol, Isla de la Luna, and Isla de la Pedrera. Group tours are also available, which often include stops at key locations, such as the Uros floating islands and the town of Copacabana, known for its beautiful church and lively waterfront.

- **Sunset Cruises:** A sunset boat cruise on Lake Titicaca is a must-do for those looking to capture the magic of the place. As the sun dips below the mountains, the shimmering waters reflect vibrant hues of orange, red, and purple, creating a picture-perfect moment. These cruises are often accompanied by local guides who share fascinating stories about the lake's history, culture, and the indigenous communities that call it home.

**Kayaking and Canoeing:** For those seeking a more active way to enjoy the lake, kayaking and canoeing are excellent options. Renting a kayak or a traditional wooden canoe from the lakeside towns of Copacabana or the islands themselves gives you the chance to navigate the tranquil waters at your own pace. This is a great way to explore smaller coves, islands, and hidden beaches that aren't accessible by larger boats. Kayaking also offers a unique opportunity to get up close to the lake's diverse wildlife, including bird species like herons, pelicans, and even the occasional Andean flamingo.

- **Lake Exploration:** Paddling around the lake gives you the chance to experience the natural beauty of Lake Titicaca from a different angle. For those who prefer a more challenging journey, guided kayaking expeditions can take you around the more remote parts of the lake, offering an adventure that combines exploration with the stunning serenity of the region. As you row through the lake's calm waters, you'll feel a profound sense of connection to the environment, making it a truly unforgettable experience.
- **Adventure and Relaxation:** While kayaking is an ideal way to explore the lake for those with a sense of adventure, it's also a relaxing activity for those who prefer a slower pace. Whether you're paddling along the shorelines or just floating lazily under the sun, kayaking offers a peaceful and meditative experience.

**Swimming and Water Sports:** Although the high altitude and chilly temperatures of Lake Titicaca might deter some from taking a dip, swimming in the lake is a refreshing experience for those who dare. The lake's crystal-clear waters are surprisingly clean, and many locals enjoy swimming in its depths. The area around Isla del Sol offers particularly inviting spots for a swim, with its warm, shallow coves and scenic surroundings. If you're adventurous, jumping off a boat into the cool waters can be invigorating, especially on a hot day.

For those who want to try something more thrilling, the lake offers opportunities for water sports such as windsurfing and stand-up paddleboarding. The surrounding wind conditions, especially on the western side of the lake near Copacabana, make it ideal for windsurfing, while the calm waters of Isla del Sol are perfect for stand-up paddleboarding.

- **Safety Precautions:** While swimming is possible, it's important to remember that the high altitude means the water is cold, and the weather conditions can change rapidly. Be sure to follow local guidelines and be cautious of your surroundings. Many tour companies that offer water activities also provide safety equipment and guidance to ensure a safe and enjoyable experience.

**Visiting Uros Floating Islands:** A visit to the Uros Islands, one of the most unique experiences on Lake Titicaca, is an absolute must. These artificial islands are constructed entirely of reeds that grow in the lake. The Uros people, an indigenous community, have lived on these floating islands for centuries. They build their islands by layering totora reeds, which are abundant in the lake, and keep the islands afloat by continually adding new layers of reeds as the old ones decay. Visiting the Uros Islands gives you a chance to learn about this incredible way of life and explore the intricate craftsmanship involved in building these floating homes.

- **Interaction with Locals:** When visiting the Uros Islands, you'll be welcomed by the locals, who are eager to share their history, traditions, and the skills required to maintain the islands. You can tour the reed houses, sample traditional foods, and even purchase handicrafts made by the Uros people. The boat ride to the islands offers a chance to see the vastness of Lake Titicaca, as well as the beautiful surrounding landscapes.

**Fishing Expeditions:** Lake Titicaca is home to a variety of fish species, including trout, which thrive in its cool, clear waters. Fishing is an important part of the local economy, particularly for the communities that live on the islands. Visitors can participate in traditional fishing expeditions, either by joining locals on their boats or hiring a guide for a more immersive experience. Fishing on Lake Titicaca is often done using traditional techniques, such as net fishing or hand lines, which allows travelers to learn about and contribute to the preservation of local practices.

- **Learning Local Techniques:** Fishing expeditions are not just about catching fish; they're also an opportunity to learn about the ancient techniques used by local fishermen. Many guides will explain how they fish according to the phases of the moon and the seasonal patterns of fish migration. These tours provide a deep dive into the sustainable fishing practices that have been passed down through generations.

**Cultural and Spiritual Activities on the Lake:** For those interested in the spiritual and cultural aspects of Lake Titicaca, there are several opportunities to participate in traditional ceremonies and rituals. In the towns and islands surrounding the lake, local shamans perform sacred ceremonies for tourists, offering blessings, healing rituals, or even performing ancient Inca rituals to honor the lake's sacred status.

- **Spiritual Connection:** Taking part in a spiritual ceremony on the shores of Lake Titicaca can be a deeply moving experience. The lake has long been regarded as a spiritual hub by the local indigenous communities, who believe it is a place of great energy. Whether you participate in a full-fledged ceremony or simply meditate by the water, the connection between the lake and the surrounding cultures is palpable and offers an enriching experience for those seeking a deeper understanding of the region's heritage.

Lake Titicaca is not just a stunning natural wonder; it's a destination filled with opportunities for adventure, relaxation, and cultural discovery. From boating and kayaking across its vast surface to visiting its floating islands and engaging in local fishing practices, there's no shortage of activities to enjoy on this mystical lake. Whether you're seeking an adrenaline rush, a cultural journey, or simply a peaceful escape into nature, Lake Titicaca promises to offer an unforgettable experience.

# CHAPTER SEVEN
# CULINARY DELIGHTS

Bolivia's culinary scene is a rich tapestry of flavors, reflecting the country's diverse landscapes and cultural influences. From the high-altitude Andes to the lush Amazon basin, the cuisine varies greatly, offering a wide range of ingredients, cooking  methods, and traditional dishes. Bolivian food is a blend of indigenous Aymara and Quechua heritage, Spanish influences, and modern touches, making every meal a unique experience. In this chapter, we will explore the vibrant flavors of Bolivia, from hearty mountain fare to exotic Amazonian specialties, each dish telling a story of the land and people who created it.

Bolivia's culinary delights are not only about taste but also about the experience. Whether you're savoring a steaming bowl of sopa de maní (peanut soup) in La Paz, enjoying a savory salteña (a Bolivian-style pastry) in Sucre, or indulging in fresh fish dishes on the shores of Lake Titicaca, the country's food is bound to leave a lasting impression. In this chapter, we'll delve into the best local dishes, regional specialties, and the best places to try them, ensuring your culinary journey through Bolivia is as unforgettable as its landscapes.

# TRADITIONAL DISHES

Bolivian cuisine is a captivating blend of indigenous ingredients and techniques influenced by centuries of cultural exchange. Rooted in the Andean, Amazonian, and colonial traditions, the food reflects the country's diverse geography and people. Each region has its own unique offerings, but there are several traditional dishes that are beloved across the country, offering an authentic taste of Bolivia's culinary identity.

**Salteñas:** One of the most iconic snacks in Bolivia, salteñas are savory pastries that resemble empanadas but with a distinct twist. These golden, flaky pastries are filled with a hearty mixture of meat (often beef or chicken), potatoes, peas, olives, and a savory broth that gives them a unique juiciness. The dish is often enjoyed for breakfast or as a mid-morning snack, making it a staple of daily life in Bolivia. The secret to the deliciousness of salteñas lies in the balance between the perfectly baked crust and the rich, flavorful filling. Eating a salteña can be an art—careful handling is required to avoid spilling the delicious broth inside!

Salteñas can be found throughout Bolivia, with each region adding its own spin. In La Paz, for instance, they are often spiced with a little more heat, while in Cochabamba, the filling may lean towards more potato-heavy ingredients. No matter where you are, salteñas offer a perfect introduction to the variety of flavors that make up Bolivian cuisine.

**Pique Macho:** A beloved Bolivian comfort food, Pique Macho is a satisfying and filling dish that packs a punch. A typical Pique Macho consists of sautéed beef (sometimes mixed with chicken or sausage), boiled potatoes, bell peppers, onions, tomatoes, and a generous sprinkling of spices. The dish is topped with hard-boiled eggs, mayonnaise, and spicy mustard, making for a hearty meal full of contrasting textures and bold flavors. It is often served on a large plate or platter, meant to be shared family-style.

Pique Macho is a popular choice for celebrations or casual gatherings and can be found at many local restaurants and street food vendors. The spicy and tangy combination of flavors, along with its filling nature, makes it a go-to dish for Bolivians who are looking for something satisfying and delicious.

**Sopa de Maní (Peanut Soup):** Sopa de Maní, or peanut soup, is one of Bolivia's most comforting and popular traditional dishes, especially in the colder high-altitude regions like La Paz. The dish is made from a creamy base of ground peanuts, which is combined with vegetables like potatoes, carrots, and onions, along with tender pieces of beef or chicken. This thick, hearty soup is often garnished with fresh herbs, such as parsley, and sometimes served with rice or corn on the side. The nutty flavor of the peanuts adds a richness that is both satisfying and warming.

Sopa de Maní is often served as a main course and is perfect for the cool evenings typical in Bolivia's Andean regions. It's a great example of how Bolivian cuisine combines indigenous ingredients with culinary influences from the Spanish, resulting in a dish that's both rich in history and flavor.

**Api con Pastel:** A traditional Bolivian drink and snack combo, Api con Pastel is often enjoyed during breakfast or as a mid-morning treat. Api is a sweet, spiced beverage made from purple corn, sugar, cloves, and cinnamon. This warm, comforting drink is thick and rich, with a flavor profile that balances sweetness and spice. The pastel (or pastry) served alongside it is a sweet, fried dough that pairs perfectly with the Api. The combination of the slightly tart, herbal drink and the sugary, crispy pastry makes for a delightful and satisfying snack.

Api con Pastel is popular in many Bolivian towns, particularly during festivals or family gatherings, where it's enjoyed as a symbol of hospitality and warmth. The purple corn used in Api is indigenous to the region and adds to the dish's distinctive color and taste. Drinking Api is not just about enjoying a beverage, it's about participating in a cultural tradition that has been passed down through generations.

**Silpancho:** Silpancho is a classic Bolivian dish that combines rice, potatoes, and breaded beef or chicken, making it a filling and well-balanced meal. The beef is thinly pounded, breaded, and fried, resulting in a crispy exterior and tender meat inside. It is served on a bed of white rice and topped with sliced potatoes and a fried egg, often accompanied by a fresh salad. The dish is commonly served with a side of llajwa, a traditional Bolivian salsa made from tomatoes, onions, and chili peppers, giving the dish an extra kick of flavor.

Silpancho is popular in the city of Cochabamba but can be found throughout Bolivia. Its combination of fried meat, rice, and potatoes reflects the Bolivian love for hearty, comforting meals that showcase the country's agricultural richness.

**Charquekan:** Charquekan is a traditional Bolivian dish that features dried, salted meat (usually llama or beef) served with roasted corn, potatoes, and sometimes a fried egg on top. The dried meat is rehydrated and then cooked, resulting in a flavorful, chewy texture that pairs beautifully with the starchy corn and potatoes. It's a dish that was originally created by indigenous communities in the Andean highlands, where dried meat was a practical and essential food preservation method for long journeys.

Charquekan is particularly popular in Bolivia's high-altitude regions and is often enjoyed as a main meal for lunch or dinner. The dish is hearty and offers a perfect mix of savory and salty flavors, making it a favorite for locals and visitors alike.

**Chairo:** A traditional Andean soup, Chairo is a deeply flavorful, hearty dish often served as a remedy for the cold. It is made with a base of beef or lamb, along with potatoes, chuño (freeze-dried potatoes), carrots, and herbs. The addition of quinoa and corn adds depth and richness to the soup. The distinct, earthy flavor of the chuño gives Chairo a unique taste, reflective of Bolivia's indigenous agricultural practices.

This dish has deep historical roots and is considered a healing food, traditionally eaten by Bolivians to restore energy after a long day of work or to combat the cold, high-altitude climate. Chairo is typically served with a side of bread or rice, making it a filling and nourishing meal for any occasion.

Bolivian cuisine is a vibrant reflection of the country's diverse landscapes, cultures, and history. From hearty comfort foods like Pique Macho and Sopa de Maní to the more refreshing Api con Pastel, every dish tells a unique story of the land and people who created it. The use of indigenous ingredients such as quinoa, potatoes, and corn, along with techniques passed down through generations, creates an unforgettable culinary experience for anyone traveling through Bolivia. Each bite offers a taste of the country's rich heritage and the warmth of its people.

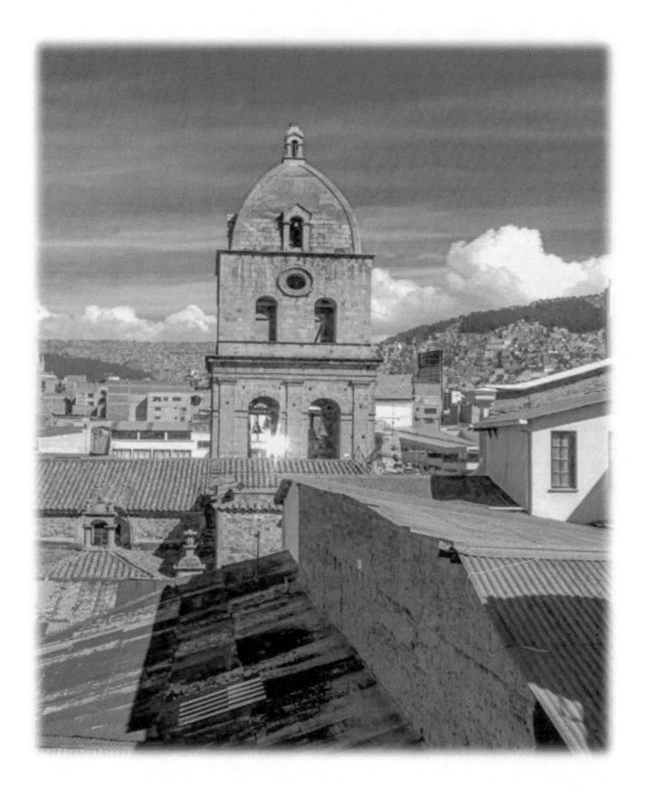

# DINING CUSTOMS

Bolivian dining customs are a reflection of the country's rich cultural heritage, shaped by its indigenous roots, colonial history, and diverse geographical regions. Food plays a central role in everyday life, and meals are often seen as a time for family and community to come together. Dining customs can vary from region to region, but there are certain traditions and practices that are common throughout the country, providing a unique and authentic experience for those who visit. Understanding these customs will not only enhance your dining experience but also give you a deeper insight into Bolivian culture.

**Meal Times and Structure:** In Bolivia, meal times tend to follow the typical South American schedule, with breakfast, lunch, and dinner being the main meals of the day. Breakfast is typically light, often consisting of bread with cheese or jam, accompanied by coffee or tea. It's a quick and simple meal, eaten at home or on the go. However, lunch is the most important and substantial meal of the day. Typically served around 1:00 PM to 2:00 PM, it consists of a multi-course meal with a soup or appetizer followed by a main dish of meat, rice, potatoes, and vegetables. Many restaurants or families also include a dessert at the end of the meal. This is often a time for people to take a break from their daily activities and enjoy a leisurely meal with family, colleagues, or friends.

Dinner in Bolivia is usually a lighter meal, served around 7:00 PM to 8:00 PM. It is often smaller than lunch and might consist of leftovers from the midday meal or a simple dish such as empanadas, tamales, or a salad with bread. While dinner is generally a less elaborate affair, it is still enjoyed as a family event, and the atmosphere is one of relaxation after a busy day.

**The Importance of Sharing Meals:** One of the key aspects of Bolivian dining culture is the importance of sharing meals. Whether in a family setting or at a social gathering, food is often served in large quantities to ensure that everyone can enjoy the meal together. It is common to see large communal plates filled with dishes like Pique Macho or Salteñas, where everyone digs in and shares the meal. In Bolivian culture, this communal aspect reflects the values of community, family, and hospitality.

For example, a typical family-style lunch might feature a large platter of Silpancho (breaded meat, potatoes, rice, and a fried egg), where family members serve themselves and pass around different sides. It's a moment of connection, where conversation and bonding flow as freely as the food. When dining at a friend's house or attending a special event, it's common to be offered a plate of food, and declining it can be considered impolite. Bolivians are known for their hospitality, and refusing an offer of food might be seen as a sign of disrespect.

**Eating Etiquette:** Bolivian dining etiquette is relatively informal, especially in the context of family meals and casual gatherings. However, there are still some customs to keep in mind to ensure respect for the host and local traditions. It is common for people to eat with a spoon for soups, stews, and other liquid-based dishes. Forks and knives are typically used for meat dishes, especially when they are served with rice or potatoes. Chopsticks are not used in Bolivia, and meals are rarely eaten by hand (unless you're enjoying snacks like salteñas or empanadas, which are hand-held foods).

When attending a formal meal or eating at a restaurant, it's customary to wait for the host to begin eating before you start your meal. As a sign of respect, you should also finish your food or at least eat a significant portion; leaving food on the plate may be seen as wasteful. If you find that you've had enough to eat, it's polite to make it clear to your host or waiter in a respectful manner rather than leaving food uneaten.

**The Role of Beverages:** In Bolivia, beverages play a vital role in the dining experience, and many meals are complemented with refreshing drinks that are both traditional and unique to the country. One of the most popular drinks is Api, a sweet, warm beverage made from purple corn, sugar, and spices such as cinnamon and cloves. Api is often enjoyed for breakfast or as a mid-morning snack, accompanied by a freshly baked pastel (pastry). Similarly, Chicha, a fermented corn beverage, is commonly consumed in some regions, particularly in the highlands. Chicha can vary in its strength and sweetness, with different regions offering their own variations.

In the cities and larger towns, soft drinks, juice, and water are also widely available and commonly consumed with meals. During special events or celebrations, a glass of wine or beer might be offered. Pisco, a local brandy made from grapes, is another popular alcoholic drink, often sipped as an aperitif or served with meals. In more rural areas, particularly in indigenous communities, herbal teas made from native plants, such as muña (Andean mint), are also consumed for their medicinal properties.

**Street Food Culture:** Bolivian street food is an essential part of the culinary landscape, offering locals and visitors alike a chance to enjoy delicious and affordable meals on the go. Street food vendors are common in cities and towns, with a variety of stalls offering snacks and light meals such as empanadas, salteñas, tamales, and humintas (corn-based pastries). Eating street food is a popular practice, and it's considered a normal part of daily life, especially for breakfast or as a quick snack during the afternoon.

Street food vendors often sell traditional snacks made fresh on-site, and it's common to see locals gathering around small carts or food trucks to sample the offerings. The vibrant colors and smells from the food stalls make for an exciting and immersive experience, and the prices are generally affordable. Whether you're in La Paz, Cochabamba, or Sucre, there's always something tasty and authentic to try from the street vendors.

**Special Occasions and Festive Meals:** Bolivian cuisine is also heavily influenced by cultural celebrations and holidays, where certain dishes and meals are prepared to mark the occasion. Carnival is one of the most important and festive events in Bolivia, and during this time, specialty dishes such as Mazamorra (a corn-based dessert) or Sopa de Queso (cheese soup) are enjoyed with family and friends. During Christmas and New Year's, dishes like Pernil (roast pork) or Lechón (roast suckling pig) are common, often served with rice, potatoes, and a variety of salads.

Throughout the year, Bolivians gather for community feasts, particularly in rural areas, where it's customary to share large meals, often featuring traditional meats like llama, beef, or chicken, along with vegetables, corn, and potatoes. Celebrations like Independence Day (August 6) or local religious festivals are marked with abundant food, music, and dancing, making dining a central aspect of Bolivia's cultural fabric.

Dining customs in Bolivia offer an intimate view into the country's cultural richness, where food is not just sustenance but a means of connection and community. Whether enjoying a casual Pique Macho with friends or sharing a festive Carnival feast with family, Bolivians hold a deep respect for food and the role it plays in everyday life. From meal structures to the communal nature of dining, and the influence of beverages and street food, the Bolivian dining experience is as diverse and unique as the country itself. By understanding these customs, travelers can gain a deeper appreciation for the culture while enjoying the many flavors that Bolivia has to offer.

SUCRE

# CONCLUSION

Bolivia is a land of stark contrasts and profound beauty, where towering Andean peaks meet the lush Amazon rainforest, where ancient cultures thrive alongside modern developments, and where every corner tells a story of resilience and transformation. From the surreal, salt-crusted plains of Salar de Uyuni to the vibrant streets of La Paz, Bolivia offers a kaleidoscope of experiences that will leave every traveler in awe. Whether you are seeking adventure in the wilderness, immersing yourself in the rich history of ancient civilizations, or savoring the flavors of a unique culinary tradition, Bolivia welcomes you with open arms and promises to create memories that will last a lifetime.

This travel guide was crafted to offer you a comprehensive and insightful look into Bolivia's most iconic destinations, cultural gems, and off-the-beaten-path treasures. Our hope is that through these pages, you are able to navigate the country's diverse landscapes, uncover hidden wonders, and experience the warmth and hospitality of its people. Bolivia may not be as widely known as some of its South American neighbors, but it is undoubtedly one of the continent's most enchanting and rewarding destinations for those willing to explore its depths.

As you plan your journey through this extraordinary country, we encourage you to keep an open mind and embrace the unexpected. Let Bolivia's beauty, both natural and cultural, inspire your wanderlust, and let every experience be an opportunity to learn and grow. Whether you are hiking through the Amazon, witnessing the wonders of the ancient Incas, or simply sharing a meal with the locals, Bolivia will undoubtedly leave its mark on your heart.

We want to take a moment to sincerely thank you for purchasing this guide. Your decision to explore Bolivia with us means a great deal, and we hope this book has enriched your travel experience in ways both big and small. If you've found this guide helpful and inspiring, we would be incredibly grateful if you could share your thoughts with others. Your honest review helps other travelers make informed decisions and ensures that we continue to offer the most up-to-date and thorough travel advice.

Your feedback is invaluable in helping us improve, and we would be deeply appreciative of any insights you can provide. If you have enjoyed this guide, please take a moment to leave a review. Your words not only support this project but also help other adventurers who are ready to experience the magic of Bolivia for themselves.

Thank you once again for choosing to explore Bolivia. Safe travels, and may your journey be filled with unforgettable moments!

Made in the USA
Coppell, TX
09 December 2024

42039921R10060